"'I BELIEVE YOU'D BLOW OUT THE GAS IN YOUR BED-ROOM'"

Coffee and Repartee
and
The Idiot

By

John Kendrick Bangs

Illustrated

Copyright, 1893, 1895, 1899, by HARPER & BROTHERS.

All rights reserved.

TO

F. S. M.

ILLUSTRATIONS

"'I BELIEVE YOU'D BLOW OUT THE GAS IN YOUR BEDROOM'" . . . . *Frontispiece*

"'WEREN'T YOUR EARS LONG ENOUGH?'". *Facing p.* 28

"'A LITTLE GARDEN OF MY OWN, WHERE I COULD RAISE AN OCCASIONAL CAN OF TOMATOES'" . . . . " 64

"THE NUISANCE OF HAVING TO PAY" . " 110

"SHE COULD NOT POSSIBLY GET ABOARD AGAIN" . . . . " 112

"THEY ARE GIVEN TO REHEARSING AT ALL HOURS" . . . . " 132

HE COULD BE HEARD THROWING THINGS ABOUT . . . . " 150

"JANITORS HAVE TO BE SEEN TO" . . " 210

COFFEE AND REPARTEE

I

THE guests at Mrs. Smithers's high-class boarding-house for gentlemen had assembled as usual for breakfast, and in a few moments Mary, the dainty waitress, entered with the steaming coffee, the mush, and the rolls.

The School-Master, who, by-the-way, was suspected by Mrs. Smithers of having intentions, and for that reason occupied the chair nearest the lady's heart, folded up the morning paper, and placing it under him so that no one else could get it, observed, quite genially for him, "It was very wet yesterday."

"I didn't find it so," observed a young man seated half-way down the table, who was by common consent called the Idiot, because of his " views." " In fact, I was very dry yesterday. Curious thing, I'm always dry on rainy days. I am one of the kind of men who know that it is the part of wisdom to stay in when it rains, or to carry an umbrella when it is not possible to stay at home, or, having no home, like ourselves, to remain cooped up in stalls, or stalled up in coops, as you may prefer."

"You carried an umbrella, then?" observed the landlady, ignoring the Idiot's shaft at the size of her " elegant and airy apartments " with an ease born of experience.

" Yes, madame," returned the Idiot, quite unconscious of what was coming.

" Whose? " queried the lady, a sarcastic smile playing about her lips.

" That I cannot say, Mrs. Smithers," replied the Idiot, serenely, " but it is the one you usually carry."

" Your insinuation, sir," said the School-Master, coming to the landlady's rescue, " is an unworthy one. The umbrella in question is mine. It has been in my possession for five years."

" Then," replied the Idiot, unabashed, " it is time you returned it. Don't you think men's morals are rather lax in this matter of umbrellas, Mr. Whitechoker?" he added, turning from the School-Master, who began to show signs of irritation.

"Very," said the Minister, running his finger about his neck to make the collar which had been sent home from the laundry by mistake set more easily—"very lax. At the last Conference I attended, some person, forgetting his high office as a minister in the Church, walked off with my umbrella without so much as a thank you; and it was embarrassing, too, because the rain was coming down in bucketfuls."

"What did you do?" asked the landlady, sympathetically. She liked Mr. Whitechoker's sermons, and, beyond this, he was a more profitable boarder than any of the others, remaining home to luncheon every day and having to pay extra therefor.

"There was but one thing left for me to do. I took the bishop's umbrella," said Mr. Whitechoker, blushing slightly.

"But you returned it, of course?" said the Idiot.

"I intended to, but I left it on the train on my way back home the next day," replied the Clergyman, visibly embarrassed by the Idiot's unexpected cross-examination.

"It's the same way with books," put in the Bibliomaniac, an unfortunate being whose love of rare first editions had brought him down from affluence to boarding. "Many a man who wouldn't steal a dollar would run off with a book. I had a friend once who had a rare copy of *Through Africa by Daylight*. It was a beautiful book. Only twenty-five copies printed. The margins of the pages were four inches wide, and the title-page was rubricated; the frontispiece was colored by hand, and the seventeenth page had one of the most amusing typographical errors on it—"

"Was there any reading-matter in the book?" asked the Idiot, blowing softly on a hot potato that was nicely balanced on the end of his fork.

"Yes, a little; but it didn't amount to much," returned the Bibliomaniac. "It isn't as reading-matter that men like myself care for books, you know. We have a higher notion than that. It is as a specimen of the book-maker's art that we admire a chaste bit of literature like *Through Africa by Day-*

light. But, as I was saying, my friend had this book, and he'd extra-illustrated it. He had pictures from all parts of the world in it, and the book had grown from a volume of one hundred pages to four volumes of two hundred pages each."

"And it was stolen by a highly honorable friend, I suppose?" the Idiot interrupted.

"Yes, it was stolen—and my friend never knew by whom," said the Bibliomaniac.

"What?" cried the Idiot, in mock surprise. "Did you never confess?"

It was fortunate for the Idiot that the buckwheat cakes were brought on at this moment. Had there not been some diversion of that kind, it is certain that the Bibliomaniac would have assaulted him.

"It is very kind of Mrs. Smithers, I think," said the School-Master, "to provide us with such delightful cakes as these free of charge."

"Yes," said the Idiot, helping himself to six cakes. "Very kind indeed, although I must say they are extremely economical from an architectural point of view—which is to say, they are rather fuller of pores than of buckwheat. I wonder why it is," he continued, possibly to avert the landlady's retaliatory comments—"I wonder why it is that porous plasters and buckwheat cakes are so similar in appearance?"

"And so widely different in their respective effects on the system," put in a genial old gentleman who occasionally imbibed, seated next to the Idiot.

"I fail to see the similarity between a buckwheat cake and a porous plaster," said the School-Master, resolved, if possible, to embarrass the Idiot.

"You don't eh?" replied the latter. "Then it is very plain, sir, that you have never eaten a porous plaster."

To this the School-Master could find no reasonable reply, and he took refuge in silence. Mr. Whitechoker tried to look severe; the gentleman who occasionally imbibed smiled all over; the Bibliomaniac ignored the remark entirely, not having as yet forgiven the Idiot for his gross insinuation regarding his friend's *édition de luxe* of *Through Africa by Daylight;* Mary, the maid, who greatly admired the Idiot, not so much for his idiocy as for the aristocratic manner in which he carried himself, and the truly striking striped shirts he wore, left the room in a convulsion of laughter that so alarmed the cook below-stairs that the next platterful of cakes were more like tin plates than cakes; and as for Mrs. Smithers, that worthy woman was speechless with wrath. But she was not paralyzed apparently, for reaching down into her pocket she brought forth a small piece of paper, on which was written in detail the "account due" of the Idiot.

"I'd like to have this settled, sir," she said, with some asperity.

"Certainly, my dear madame," replied the Idiot, unabashed—"certainly. Can you cash a check for a hundred?"

No, Mrs. Smithers could not.

"Then I shall have to put off paying the account until this evening," said the Idiot. "But tell me," he added, with a glance at the amount of the bill, "are you related to Mr. McKinley, Mrs. Smithers?"

"I am not," she returned, sharply. "My mother was a Partington."

"I only asked," said the Idiot, apologetically, "because I am very much interested in the subject of heredity, and you may not know it, but you and he have each a marked tendency towards high-tariff bills,"

And before Mrs. Smithers could think of anything to say, the Idiot was on his way down town to help his employer lose money on Wall Street.

II

"Do you know, I sometimes think—" began the Idiot, opening and shutting the silver cover of his watch several times with a snap, with the probable, and not altogether laudable, purpose of calling his landlady's attention to the fact—of which she was already painfully aware—that breakfast was fifteen minutes late.

"Do you, really?" interrupted the School-Master, looking up from his book with an air of mock surprise. "I am sure I never should have suspected it."

"Indeed?" returned the Idiot, undisturbed by this reflection upon his intellect. "I don't really know whether that is due to your generally unsuspicious nature, or to your shortcomings as a mind-reader."

"There are some minds," put in the landlady at this point, "that are so small that it would certainly ruin the eyes to attempt to read them."

"I have seen many such," observed the Idiot, suavely. "Even our friend the Bibliomaniac at times has seemed to me to be very absent-minded. And that reminds me, Doctor," he continued, addressing himself to the medical boarder. "What is the cause of absent-mindedness?"

"That," returned the Doctor, ponderously, "is a very large question. Absent-mindedness, generally speaking, is the result of the projection of the intellect into surroundings other than those which for want of a better term I might call the corporeally immediate."

"So I have understood," said the Idiot, approvingly. "And is absent-mindedness acquired or inherent?"

Here the Idiot appropriated the roll of his neighbor.

"That depends largely upon the case," replied the Doctor, nervously. "Some are born absent-minded, some achieve absent-mindedness, and some have absent-mindedness thrust upon them."

"As illustrations of which we might take,

for instance, I suppose," said the Idiot, "the born idiot, the borrower, and the man who is knocked silly by the pole of a truck on Broadway."

"Precisely," replied the Doctor, glad to get out of the discussion so easily. He was a very young doctor, and not always sure of himself.

"Or," put in the School-Master, "to condense our illustrations, if the Idiot would kindly go out upon Broadway and encounter the truck, we should find the three combined in him."

The landlady here laughed quite heartily, and handed the School-Master an extra strong cup of coffee.

"There is a great deal in what you say," said the Idiot, without a tremor. "There are very few scientific phenomena that cannot be demonstrated in one way or another by my poor but essentially honest self. It is the exception always that proves the rule, and in my case you find a consistent converse exemplification of all three branches of absent-mindedness."

"He talks well," said the Bibliomaniac, *sotto voce,* to the Minister.

"Yes, especially when he gets hold of large words. I really believe he reads," replied Mr. Whitechoker.

"I know he does," said the School-Master, who had overheard. "I saw him reading Webster's Dictionary last night. I have noticed, however, that generally his vocabulary is largely confined to words that come between the letters A and F, which shows that as yet he has not dipped very deeply into the book."

"What are you murmuring about?" queried the Idiot, noting the lowered tone of those on the other side of the table.

"We were conversing—ahem! about—" began the Minister, with a despairing glance at the Bibliomaniac.

"Let me say it," interrupted the Bibliomaniac. "You aren't used to prevarication, and that is what is demanded at this time. We were talking about—ah—about—er—"

"Tut! tut!" ejaculated the School-Master. "We were only saying we thought the —er—the—that the—"

"What *are* the first symptoms of insanity, Doctor?" observed the Idiot, with a look of wonder at the three shuffling boarders opposite him, and turning anxiously to the physician.

"I wish you wouldn't talk shop," retorted the Doctor, angrily. Insanity was one of his weak points.

"It's a beastly habit," said the School-Master, much relieved at this turn of the conversation.

"Well, perhaps you are right," returned the Idiot. "People do, as a rule, prefer to talk of things they know something about, and I don't blame you, Doctor, for wanting to keep out of a medical discussion. I only asked my last question because the behavior of the Bibliomaniac and Mr. Whitechoker and the School-Master for some time past has worried me, and I didn't know but what you might work up a nice little practice among us. It might not pay, but you'd find the experience valuable, and I think unique."

"It is a fine thing to have a doctor right in the house," said Mr. Whitechoker, kindly, fearing that the Doctor's manifest indignation might get the better of him.

"That," returned the Idiot, "is an assertion, Mr. Whitechoker, that is both true and untrue. There are times when a physician is an ornament to a boarding-house; times when he is not. For instance, on Wednesday morning if it had not been for the surgical skill of our friend here, our good landlady could never have managed properly to distribute the late autumn chicken we found upon the menu. Tally one for the affirmative. On the other hand, I must confess to considerable loss of appetite when I see the Doctor rolling his bread up into little pills, or measuring the vinegar he puts on his salad by means of a glass dropper, and taking the temperature of his coffee with his pocket thermometer. Nor do I like—and I should not have mentioned it save by way of illustrating my position in regard to Mr. Whitechoker's assertion—nor do I like the cold, eager glitter in the Doctor's eyes as he watches me consuming, with some difficulty, I admit, the cold pastry we have served up to us on Saturday mornings under the wholly transparent *alias* of 'Hot Bread.' I may have very bad taste, but, in my humble opinion, the man who talks shop is preferable to the one who suggests it in his eyes. Some more iced potatoes, Mary," he added, calmly.

"Madame," said the Doctor, turning angrily to the landlady, "this is insufferable. You may make out my bill this morning. I shall have to seek a home elsewhere."

"Oh, now, Doctor!" began the landlady, in her most pleading tone.

"Jove!" ejaculated the Idiot. "That's a good idea, Doctor. I think I'll go with you. I'm not altogether satisfied here myself, but to desert so charming a company as we have here had never occurred to me. Together, however, we can go forth, and perhaps find happiness. Shall we put on our hunting togs and chase the fiery, untamed hall-room to the death this morning, or shall we put it off until some pleasanter day?"

"Put it off," observed the School-Master, persuasively. "The Idiot was only indulging in persiflage, Doctor. That's all. When you have known him longer you will understand him better. Views are as necessary to him as sunlight to the flowers; and I truly think that in an asylum he would prove a delightful companion."

"There, Doctor," said the Idiot; "that's handsome of the School-Master. He couldn't make more of an apology if he tried. I'll forgive him if you will. What say you?"

And strange to say, the Doctor, in spite of the indignation which still left a red tinge on his cheek, laughed aloud and was reconciled.

As for the School-Master, he wanted to be angry, but he did not feel that he could afford his wrath, and for the first time in some months the guests went their several ways at peace with each other and the world.

III

THERE was a conspiracy in hand to embarrass the Idiot. The School-Master and the Bibliomaniac had combined forces to give him a taste of his own medicine. The time had not yet arrived which showed the Idiot at a disadvantage; and the two boarders, the one proud of his learning, and the other not wholly unconscious of a bookish life, were distinctly tired of the triumphant manner in which the Idiot always left the breakfast-table to their invariable discomfiture.

It was the School-Master's suggestion to put their tormentor into the pit he had heretofore digged for them. The worthy instructor of youth had of late come to see that while he was still a prime favorite with his landlady, he had, nevertheless, suffered somewhat in her estimation because of the apparent ease with which the Idiot had got the better of him on all points. It was necessary, he thought, to rehabilitate himself, and a deep-laid plot, to which the Bibliomaniac readily lent ear, was the result of his reflections. They twain were to indulge in a discussion of the great story of *Robert Elsmere,* which both were confident the Idiot had not read, and concerning which they felt assured he could not have an intelligent opinion if he had read it.

So it happened upon this bright Sunday morning that as the boarders sat them down to partake of the usual " restful breakfast," as the Idiot termed it, the Bibliomaniac observed :

" I have just finished reading *Robert Elsmere.*"

" Have you, indeed?" returned the School-Master, with apparent interest. " I trust you profited by it ? "

" On the contrary," observed the Bibliomaniac. " My views are much unsettled by it."

" I prefer the breast of the chicken, Mrs. Smithers," observed the Idiot, sending his plate back to the presiding genius of the table. " The neck of a chicken is graceful, but not too full of sustenance."

"He fights shy," whispered the Bibliomaniac, gleefully.

"Never mind," returned the School-Master, confidently; "we'll land him yet." Then he added, aloud: "Unsettled by it? I fail to see how any man with beliefs that are at all the result of mature convictions can be unsettled by the story of *Elsmere*. For my part I believe, and I have always said—"

"I never could understand why the neck of a chicken should be allowed on a respectable table anyhow," continued the Idiot, ignoring the controversy in which his neighbors were engaged, "unless for the purpose of showing that the deceased fowl met with an accidental rather than a natural death."

"In what way does the neck demonstrate that point?" queried the Bibliomaniac, forgetting the conspiracy for a moment.

"By its twist or by its length, of course," returned the Idiot. "A chicken that dies a natural death does not have its neck wrung; nor when the head is removed by the use of a hatchet, is it likely that it will be cut off so close behind the ears that those who eat the chicken are confronted with four inches of neck."

"Very entertaining indeed," interposed the School-Master; "but we are wandering from the point the Bibliomaniac and I were discussing. Is or is not the story of *Robert Elsmere* unsettling to one's beliefs? Perhaps you can help us to decide that question."

"Perhaps I can," returned the Idiot; "and perhaps not. It did not unsettle my beliefs."

"But don't you think," observed the Bibliomaniac, "that to certain minds the book is more or less unsettling?"

"To that I can confidently say no. The certain mind knows no uncertainty," replied the Idiot, calmly.

"Very pretty indeed," said the School-Master, coldly. "But what was your opinion of Mrs. Ward's handling of the subject? Do you think she was sufficiently realistic? And if so, and Elsmere weakened under the stress of circumstances, do you think—or don't you think—the production of such a book harmful, because—being real—it must of necessity therefore be unsettling to some minds?"

"I prefer not to express an opinion on

that subject," returned the Idiot, "because I never read *Robert Els*—"

"Never read it?" ejaculated the School-Master, a look of triumph in his eyes.

"Why, everybody has read *Elsmere* that pretends to have read anything," asserted the Bibliomaniac.

"Of course," put in the landlady, with a scornful laugh.

"Well, I didn't," said the Idiot, nonchalantly. "The same ground was gone over two years before in Burrows's great story, *Is It, or Is It Not?* and anybody who ever read Clink's books on the *Non-Existent as Opposed to What Is,* knows where Burrows got his points. Burrows's story was a perfect marvel. I don't know how many editions it went through in England, and when it was translated into French by Madame Tournay, it simply set France wild."

"Great Scott!" whispered the Bibliomaniac, desperately, "I'm afraid we've been barking up the wrong tree."

"You've read Clink, I suppose?" asked the Idiot, turning to the School-Master.

"Y—es," returned the School-Master, blushing deeply.

The Idiot looked surprised, and tried to conceal a smile by sipping his coffee from a spoon.

"And Burrows?"

"No," returned the School-Master, humbly. "I never read Burrows."

"Well, you ought to. It's a great book, and it's the one *Robert Elsmere* is taken from—same ideas all through, I'm told—that's why I didn't read *Elsmere*. Waste of time, you know. But you noticed yourself, I suppose, that Clink's ground is the same as that covered in *Elsmere?*"

"No; I only dipped lightly into Clink," returned the School-Master, with some embarrassment.

"But you couldn't help noticing a similarity of ideas?" insisted the Idiot, calmly.

The School-Master looked beseechingly at the Bibliomaniac, who would have been glad to fly to his co-conspirator's assistance had he known how, but never having heard of Clink, or Burrows either, for that matter, he made up his mind that it was best for his reputation for him to stay out of the controversy.

"Very slight similarity, however," said the School-Master, in despair.

"Where can I find Clink's books?" put in Mr. Whitechoker, very much interested.

The Idiot conveniently had his mouth full of chicken at the moment, and it was to the School-Master, who had also read him, that they all—the landlady included—looked for an answer.

"Oh, I think," returned that worthy, hesitatingly—"I think you'll find Clink in any of the public libraries."

"What is his full name?" persisted Mr. Whitechoker, taking out a memorandum-book.

"Horace J. Clink," said the Idiot.

"Yes; that's it—Horace J. Clink," echoed the School-Master. "Very virile writer and a clear thinker," he added, with some nervousness.

"What, if any, of his books would you specially recommend?" asked the Minister again.

The Idiot had by this time risen from the table, and was leaving the room with the genial gentleman who occasionally imbibed.

The School-Master's reply was not audible.

"I say," said the genial gentleman to the

Idiot as they passed out into the hall, "they didn't get much the best of you in that matter. But, tell me, who was Clink, anyhow?"

"Never heard of him before," returned the Idiot.

"And Burrows?"

"Same as Clink."

"Know anything about *Elsmere*?" chuckled the genial gentleman.

"Nothing—except that it and 'Pigs in Clover' came out at the same time, and I stuck to the Pigs."

And the genial gentleman who occasionally imbibed was so pleased at the plight of the School-Master and of the Bibliomaniac that he invited the Idiot up to his room, where the private stock was kept for just such occasions, and they put in a very pleasant morning together.

IV.

THE guests were assembled as usual. The oatmeal course had been eaten in silence. In the Idiot's eye there was a cold glitter of expectancy—a glitter that boded ill for the man who should challenge him to controversial combat—and there seemed also to be, judging from sundry winks passed over the table and kicks passed under it, an understanding to which he and the genial gentleman who occasionally imbibed were parties.

As the School-Master sampled his coffee the genial gentleman who occasionally imbibed broke the silence.

"I missed you at the concert last night, Mr. Idiot," said he.

"Yes," said the Idiot, with a caressing movement of the hand over his upper lip; "I was very sorry, but I couldn't get around last night. I had an engagement with a number of friends at the athletic club. I meant to have dropped you a line in the afternoon telling you about it, but I forgot it until it was too late. Was the concert a success?"

"Very successful indeed. The best one, in fact, we have had this season, which makes me regret all the more deeply your absence," returned the genial gentleman, with a suggestion of a smile playing about his lips. "Indeed," he added, "it was the finest one I've ever seen."

"The finest one you've what?" queried the School-Master, startled at the verb.

"The finest one I've ever seen," replied the genial gentleman. "There were only ten performers, and really, in all my experience as an attendant at concerts, I never saw such a magnificent rendering of Beethoven as we had last night. I wish you could have been there. It was a sight for the gods."

"I don't believe," said the Idiot, with a slight cough that may have been intended to conceal a laugh—and that may also have been the result of too many cigarettes—"I don't believe it could have been any more interesting than a game of pool I heard at the club."

"It appears to me," said the Bibliomaniac to the School-Master, "that the popping sounds we heard late last night in the Idiot's room may have some connection with the present mode of speech these two gentlemen affect."

"Let's hear them out," returned the School-Master, "and then we'll take them into camp, as the Idiot would say."

"I don't know about that," replied the genial gentleman. "I've seen a great many concerts, and I've heard a great many good games of pool, but the concert last night was simply a ravishing spectacle. We had a Cuban pianist there who played the orchestration of the first act of *Parisfal* with surprising agility. As far as I could see, he didn't miss a note, though it was a little annoying to observe how inadequately he used the pedals."

"Too forcibly, or how?" queried the Idiot.

"Not forcibly enough," returned the Imbiber. "He tried to work them both with one foot. It was the only thing to mar an otherwise marvellous performance. The idea of a man trying to display Wagner with two hands and one foot is irritating to a musician with a trained eye."

"I wish the Doctor would come down," said Mrs. Smithers, anxiously.

"Yes," put in the School-Master; "there seems to be madness in our midst."

"Well, what can you expect of a Cuban, anyhow?" queried the Idiot. "The Cuban, like the Spaniard or the Italian or the African, hasn't the vigor which is necessary for the proper comprehension and rendering of Wagner's music. He is by nature slow and indolent. If it were easier for a Spaniard to hop than to walk, he'd hop, and rest his other leg. I've known Italians whose diet was entirely confined to liquids, because they were too tired to masticate solids. It is the ease with which it can be absorbed that makes macaroni the favorite dish of the Italians, and the fondness of all Latin races for wines is entirely due, I think, to the fact that wine can be swallowed without chewing. This indolence affects also their language. The Italian and the Spaniard speak the language that comes easy—that is soft and dreamy; while the Germans and Russians, stronger, more energetic, indulge in a speech

"'WEREN'T YOUR EARS LONG ENOUGH?'"

that even to us, who are people of an average amount of energy, is sometimes appalling in the severity of the strain it puts upon the tongue. So, while I do not wonder that your Cuban pianist showed woful defects in his use of the pedals, I do wonder that, even with his surprising agility, he had sufficient energy to manipulate the keys to the satisfaction of so competent a witness as yourself."

"It was too bad; but we made up for it later," asserted the other. "There was a young girl there who gave us some of Mendelssohn's Songs without Words. Her expression was simply perfect. I wouldn't have missed it for all the world; and now that I think of it, in a few days I can let you see for yourself how splendid it was. We persuaded her to encore the songs in the dark, and we got a flash-light photograph of two of them."

"Oh! then it was not on the piano-forte she gave them?" said the Idiot.

"Oh no; all labial," returned the genial gentleman.

Here Mr. Whitechoker began to look concerned, and whispered something to the

School-Master, who replied that there were enough others present to cope with the two parties to the conversation in case of a violent outbreak.

"I'd be very glad to see the photographs," replied the Idiot. "Can't I secure copies of them for my collection? You know I have the complete rendering of 'Home, Sweet Home' in kodak views, as sung by Patti. They are simply wonderful, and they prove what has repeatedly been said by critics, that, in the matter of expression, the superior of Patti has never been seen."

"I'll try to get them for you, though I doubt it can be done. The artist is a very shy young girl, and does not care to have her efforts given too great a publicity until she is ready to go into music a little more deeply. She is going to read the 'Moonlight Sonata' to us at our next concert. You'd better come. I'm told her gestures bring out the composer's meaning in a manner never as yet equalled."

"I'll be there; thank you," returned the Idiot. "And the next time those fellows at the club are down for a pool tournament I want you to come up and hear them play.

It was extraordinary last night to hear the balls dropping one by one—click, click, click—as regularly as a metronome, into the pockets. One of the finest shots, I am sorry to say, I missed."

"How did it happen?" asked the Bibliomaniac. "Weren't your ears long enough?"

"It was a kiss shot, and I couldn't hear it," returned the Idiot.

"I think you men are crazy," said the School-Master, unable to contain himself any longer.

"So?" observed the Idiot, calmly. "And how do we show our insanity?"

"Seeing concerts and hearing games of pool."

"I take exception to your ruling," returned the Imbiber. "As my friend the Idiot has frequently remarked, you have the peculiarity of a great many men in your profession, who think because they never happened to see or do or hear things as other people do, they may not be seen, done, or heard at all. I *saw* the concert I attended last night. Our musical club has rooms next to a hospital, and we have to give silent concerts for fear of disturbing the patients; but we are all musicians of sufficient education to understand by a glance of the eye what you would fail to comprehend with fourteen ears and a microphone."

"Very well said," put in the Idiot, with a scornful glance at the School-Master. "And I literally heard the pool tournament. I was dining in a room off the billiard-hall, and every shot that was made, with the exception of the one I spoke of, was distinctly audible. You gentlemen, who think you know it all, wouldn't be able to supply a bureau of information at the rate of five minutes a day for an hour on a holiday. Let's go up-stairs," he added, turning to the Imbiber, "where we may discuss our last night's entertainment apart from this atmosphere of rarefied learning. It makes me faint."

And the Imbiber, who was with difficulty keeping his lips in proper form, was glad enough to accept the invitation. "The corks popped to some purpose last night," he said, later on.

"Yes," said the Idiot; "for a conspiracy there's nothing so helpful as popping corks."

V

"When you get through with the fire, Mr. Pedagog," observed the Idiot, one winter's morning, observing that the ample proportions of the School-Master served as a screen to shut off the heat from himself and the genial gentleman who occasionally imbibed, "I wish you would let us have a little of it. Indeed, if you could conveniently spare so little as one flame for my friend here and myself, we'd be much obliged."

"It won't hurt you to cool off a little, sir," returned the School-Master sarcastically and without moving.

"No, I am not so much afraid of the injury that may be mine as I am concerned for you. If that fire should melt our only refrigerating material, I do not know what our good landlady would do. Is it true, as the Bibliomaniac asserts, that Mrs. Smithers leaves all her milk and butter in your room overnight, relying upon your coolness to keep them fresh?"

"I never made any such assertion," said the Bibliomaniac, warmly.

"I am not used to having my word disputed," returned the Idiot, with a wink at the genial old gentleman.

"But I never said it, and I defy you to prove that I said it," returned the Bibliomaniac, hotly.

"You forget, sir," said the Idiot, coolly, "that you are the one who disputes my assertion. That casts the burden of proof on your shoulders. Of course if you can prove that you never said anything of the sort, I withdraw; but if you cannot adduce proofs, you, having doubted my word, and publicly at that, need not feel hurt if I decline to accept all that you say as gospel."

"You show ridiculous heat," said the School-Master.

"Thank you," returned the Idiot, gracefully. "And that brings us back to the original proposition that you would do well to show a little yourself."

"Good-morning, gentlemen," said Mrs.

Smithers, entering the room at this moment. "It's a bright, fresh morning."

"Like yourself," said the School-Master, gallantly.

"Yes," added the Idiot, with a glance at the clock, which registered 8.45—forty-five minutes after the breakfast hour—"very like Mrs. Smithers—rather advanced."

To this the landlady paid no attention; but the School-Master could not refrain from saying:

"Advanced, and therefore not backward, like some persons I might name."

"Very clever," retorted the Idiot, "and really worth rewarding. Mrs. Smithers, you ought to give Mr. Pedagog a receipt in full for the past six months."

"Mr. Pedagog," returned the landlady, severely, "is one of the gentlemen who always have their receipts for the past six months."

"Which betrays a very saving disposition," accorded the Idiot. "I wish I had all I'd received for six months. I'd be a rich man."

"Would you, now?" queried the Bibliomaniac. "That is interesting enough. How men's ideas differ on the subject of wealth!

Here is the Idiot would consider himself rich with $150 in his pocket—"

"Do you think he gets as much as that?" put in the School-Master, viciously. "Five dollars a week is rather high pay for one of his—"

"Very high indeed," agreed the Idiot. "I wish I got that much. I might be able to hire a two-legged encyclopædia to tell me everything, and have over $4.75 a week left to spend on opera, dress, and the poor but honest board Mrs. Smithers provides, if my salary was up to the $5 mark; but the trouble is men do not make the fabulous fortunes nowadays with the ease with which you, Mr. Pedagog, made yours. There are, no doubt, more and greater opportunities to-day than there were in the olden time, but there are also more men trying to take advantage of them. Labor in the business world is badly watered. The colleges are turning out more men in a week nowadays than the whole country turned out in a year forty years ago, and the quality is so poor that there has been a general reduction of wages all along the line. Where does the struggler for existence come in when he has to compete with the college-bred youth who, for fear of not getting employment anywhere, is willing to work for nothing? People are not willing to pay for what they can get for nothing."

"I am glad to hear from your lips so complete an admission," said the School-Master, "that education is downing ignorance."

"I am glad to know of your gladness," returned the Idiot. "I didn't quite say that education was downing ignorance. I plead guilty to the charge of holding the belief that unskilled omniscience interferes very materially with skilled sciolism in skilled sciolism's efforts to make a living."

"Then you admit your own superficiality?" asked the School-Master, somewhat surprised by the Idiot's command of syllables.

"I admit that I do not know it all," returned the Idiot. "I prefer to go through life feeling that there is yet something for me to learn. It seems to me far better to admit this voluntarily than to have it forced home upon me by circumstances, as happened in the case of a college graduate I know, who speculated on Wall Street, and lost the hundred dollars that were subsequently put to a good use by the uneducated me."

"From which you deduce that ignorance is better than education?" queried the School-Master, scornfully.

"For an omniscient," returned the Idiot, "you are singularly near-sighted. I have made no such deduction. I arrive at the conclusion, however, that in the chase for the gilded shekel the education of experience is better than the coddling of Alma Mater. In the satisfaction—the personal satisfaction—one derives from a liberal education, I admit that the sons of Alma Mater are the better off. I never could hope to be so self-satisfied, for instance, as you are."

"No," observed the School-Master; "you cannot raise grapes on a thistle farm. Any unbiassed observer looking around this table," he added, "and noting Mr. Whitechoker, a graduate of Yale; the Bibliomaniac, a son of dear old Harvard; the Doctor, an honor man of Williams; our legal friend here, a graduate of Columbia—to say nothing of myself, who was graduated with honors at Amherst —any unbiassed observer seeing these, I say, and then seeing you, wouldn't take very long to make up his mind as to whether a man is better off or not for having had a collegiate training."

"There I must again dispute your assertion," returned the Idiot. "The unbiassed person of whom you speak would say, 'Here is this gray-haired Amherst man, this book-loving Cambridge boy of fifty-seven years of age, the reverend graduate of Yale, class of '55, and the other two learned gentlemen of forty-nine summers each, and this poor ignoramus of an Idiot, whose only virtue is his modesty, all in the same box.' And then he would ask himself, 'In what way have these lusty sons of Amherst, Yale, Harvard, and so forth, the better of the modest and unassuming Idiot?'"

"The same box?" said the Bibliomaniac. "What do you mean by that?"

"Just what I say," returned the Idiot. "The same box. All boarding, all eschewing luxuries of necessity, all paying their bills with difficulty, all sparsely clothed; in reality, all keeping Lent the year through. 'Verily,' he would say, 'the Idiot has the best of it, for he is young.'"

And leaving them chewing the cud of reflection, the Idiot departed.

"I thought they were going to land you that time," said the genial gentleman who occasionally imbibed, later; "but when I heard you use the word 'sciolism,' I knew you were all right. Where did you get it?"

"My chief got it off on me at the office the other day. I happened in a mad moment to try to unload some of my original observations on him apropos of my getting to the office two hours late, in which it was my endeavor to prove to him that the truly safe and conservative man was always slow, and so apt to turn up late on occasions. He hopped about the office for a minute or two, and then he informed me that I was an 18-karat sciolist. I didn't know what he meant, and so I looked it up."

"And what did he mean?"

"He meant that I took the cake for superficiality, and I guess he was right," replied the Idiot, with a smile that was not altogether mirthful.

VI

"GOOD-MORNING!" said the Idiot, cheerfully, as he entered the dining-room.

To this remark no one but the landlady vouchsafed a reply. "I don't think it is," she said, shortly. "It's raining too hard to be a very good morning."

"That reminds me," observed the Idiot, taking his seat and helping himself copiously to the hominy. "A friend of mine on one of the newspapers is preparing an article on the 'Antiquity of Modern Humor.' With your kind permission, Mrs. Smithers, I'll take down your remark and hand it over to Mr. Scribuler as a specimen of the modern antique joke. You may not be aware of the fact, but that jest is to be found in the rare first edition of the *Tales of Bobbo*, an Italian humorist, who stole everything he wrote from the Greeks."

"So?" queried the Bibliomaniac. "I never heard of Bobbo, though I had, before the auction sale of my library, a choice copy of the *Tales of Poggio,* bound in full crushed Levant morocco, with gilt edges; and one or two other Italian *Joe Millers* in tree calf. I cannot at this moment recall their names."

"At what period did Bobbo live?" inquired the School-Master.

"I don't exactly remember," returned the Idiot, assisting the last potato on the table over to his plate. "I don't know exactly. It was subsequent to B.C., I think, although I may be wrong. If it was not, you may rest assured it was prior to B.C."

"Do you happen to know," queried the Bibliomaniac, "the exact date of this rare first edition of which you speak?"

"No; no one knows that," returned the Idiot. "And for a very good reason. It was printed before dates were invented."

The silence which followed this bit of information from the Idiot was almost insulting in its intensity. It was a silence that spoke, and what it said was that the Idiot's idiocy was colossal, and he, accepting the stillness as a tribute, smiled sweetly.

"What do you think, Mr. White-choker," he said, when he thought the time was ripe for renewing the conversation—"what do you think of the doctrine that every day will be Sunday by-and-by?"

"I have only to say, sir," returned the Dominie, pouring a little hot water into his milk, which was a bit too strong for him, "that I am a firm believer in the occurrence of a period when Sunday will be to all practical purposes perpetual."

"That is my belief, too," observed the School-Master. "But it will be ruinous to our good landlady to provide us with one of her exceptionally fine Sunday breakfasts every morning."

"Thank you, Mr. Pedagog," returned

BOBBO

Mrs. Smithers, with a smile. "Can't I give you another cup of coffee?"

"You may," returned the School-Master, pained at the lady's grammar, but too courteous to call attention to it save by the emphasis with which he spoke the word "may."

"That's one view to take of it," said the Idiot. "But in case we got a Sunday breakfast every day in the week, we, on the other hand, would get approximately what we pay for. You may fill my cup too, Mrs. Smithers."

"The coffee is all gone," returned the landlady, with a snap.

"Then, Mary," said the Idiot, gracefully, turning to the maid, "you may give me a glass of ice-water. It is quite as warm, after all, as the coffee, and not quite so weak. A perpetual Sunday, though, would have its drawbacks," he added, unconscious of the venomous glances of the landlady. "You, Mr. Whitechoker, for instance, would be preaching all the time, and in consequence would soon break down. Then the effect upon our eyes from habitually reading the Sunday newspapers day after day would be extremely bad; nor must we forget that an eternity of Sundays means the elimination 'from our midst,' as the novelists say, of baseball, of circuses, of horse-racing, and other necessities of life, unless we are prepared to cast over the Puritanical view of Sunday which now prevails. It would substitute Dr. Watts for 'Annie Rooney.' We should lose 'Ta-ra-ra-boom-de-ay' entirely, which is a point in its favor."

"I don't know about that," said the genial old gentleman. "I rather like that song."

"Did you ever hear me sing it?" asked the Idiot.

"Never mind," returned the genial old gentleman, hastily. "Perhaps you are right, after all."

The Idiot smiled, and resumed: "Our shops would be perpetually closed, and an enormous loss to the shopkeepers would be sure to follow. Mr. Pedagog's theory that we should have Sunday breakfasts every day is not tenable, for the reason that with a perpetual day of rest agriculture would die out, food products would be killed off by unpulled weeds; in fact, we should go back to that really unfortunate period when women were without dress-makers, and man's chief object in life was to christen animals as he met them, and to abstain from apples, wisdom, and full dress."

"The Idiot is right," said the Bibliomaniac. "It would not be a very good thing for the world if every day were Sunday. Wash-day is a necessity of life. I am willing to admit this, in the face of the fact that wash-day meals are invariably atrocious. Contracts would be void, as a rule, because Sunday is a *dies non.*"

"A what?" asked the Idiot.

"A non-existent day in a business sense," put in the School-Master.

"Of course," said the landlady, scornfully. "Any person who knows anything knows that."

"Then, madame," returned the Idiot, rising from his chair, and putting a handful of sweet crackers in his pocket—"then I must put in a claim for $104 from you, having been charged at the rate of one dollar a day for 104 *dies nons* in the two years I have been with you."

"Indeed!" returned the lady, sharply. "Very well. And I shall put in a counter-claim for the lunches you carry away from the breakfast table every morning in your pockets."

"In that event we'll call it off, madame," returned the Idiot, as with a courtly bow and a pleasant smile he left the room.

"Well, I call him 'off,'" was all the landlady could say, as the other guests took their departure.

And of course the School-Master agreed with her.

VII

"Our streets appear to be as far from perfect as ever," said the Bibliomaniac with a sigh, as he looked out through the window at the great pools of water that gathered in the basins made by the sinking of the Belgian blocks. "We'd better go back to the cowpaths of our fathers."

"There is a great deal in what you say," observed the School-Master. "The cowpath has all the solidity of mother earth, and none of the distracting noises we get from the pavements that obtain to-day. It is porous and absorbs the moisture. The Belgian pavement is leaky, and lets it run into our cellars. We might do far worse than to go back—"

"Excuse me for having an opinion," said the Idiot, "but the man of enterprise can't afford to indulge in the luxury of the somnolent cowpath. It is too quiet. It conduces to sleep, which is a luxury business men cannot afford to indulge in too freely. Man must be up and doing. The prosperity of a great city is to my mind directly due to its noise and clatter, which effectually put a stop to napping, and keep men at all times wide awake."

"This is a Welsh-rabbit idea, I fancy," said the School-Master, quietly. He had overheard the Idiot's confidences, as revealed to the genial Imbiber, regarding the sources of some of his ideas.

"Not at all," returned the Idiot. "These ideas are beef—not Welsh-rabbit. They are the result of much thought. If you will put your mind on the subject, you will see for yourself that there is more in my theory than there is in yours. The prosperity of a locality is the greater as the noise in its vicinity increases. It is in the quiet neighborhood that man stagnates. Where do we find great business houses? Where do we find great fortunes made? Where do we find the busy bees who make the honey that enables posterity to get into Society and do nothing? Do we pick up our millions on the cowpath? I guess not. Do we erect our most princely business houses along the roads laid out by our bovine sister? I think not. Does the man who goes from the towpath to the White House take the short cut? I fancy not. He goes over the block pavement. He seeks the home of the noisy, clattering street before he lands in the shoes of Washington. The man who sticks to the cowpath may be able to drink milk, but he never wears diamonds."

"All that you say is very true, but it is not based on any fundamental principle. It is so because it happens to be so," returned the School-Master. "If it were man's habit to have the streets laid out on the old cowpath principle in his cities he would be quite as energetic, quite as prosperous, as he is now."

"No fundamental principle involved? There is the fundamental principle of all business success involved," said the Idiot, warming up to his subject. "What is the basic quality in the good business man? Alertness. What is 'alertness'? Wide-awakeishness. In this town it is impossible for a man to sleep after a stated hour, and for no other reason than that the clatter of the pavements prevents him. As a promoter of alertness, where is your cowpath? The cowpaths of the Catskills, and we all know the mountains are riddled by 'em, didn't keep Rip Van Winkle awake, and I'll wager Mr. Whitechoker here a year's board that there isn't a man in his congregation who can sleep a half-hour—much less twenty years—with Broadway within hearing distance.

"I tell you, Mr. Pedagog," he continued, "it is the man from the cowpath who gets buncoed. It's the man from the cowpath who can't make a living even out of what he calls his 'New York Store.' It is the man from the cowpath who rejoices because he can sell ten dollars' worth of sheep's-wool for five dollars, and is happy when he goes to meeting dressed up in a four-dollar suit of clothes that has cost him twenty."

"Your theory, my young friend," observed the School-Master, "is as fragile as this cup"—tapping his coffee-cup. "The countryman of whom you speak is up and doing long before you or I or your successful merchant, who has waxed great on noise as you put it, is awake. If the early bird catches the worm, what becomes of your theory?"

"The early bird does get the bait," replied the Idiot. "But he does not catch the fish, and I'll offer the board another wager that the Belgian block merchant is wider awake at 8 A.M., when he first opens his eyes, than his suburban brother who gets up at five is all day. It's the extent to which the eyes are opened that counts, and as for your statement that the fact that prosperity and noisy streets go hand in hand is true only because it happens to be so, that is an argument which may be applied to any truth in existence. I am because I happen to be, not because I am. You are what you are because you are, because if you were not, you would not be what you are."

"Your logic is delightful," said the School-Master, scornfully.

"I strive to please," replied the Idiot. "But I do agree with the Bibliomaniac that our streets are far from perfection," he added. "In my opinion they should be laid in strata. On the ground-floor should be the sewers and telegraph pipes; above this should be the water-mains; then a layer for trucks;

then a broad stratum for carriages, above which should be a promenade for pedestrians. The promenade for pedestrians should be divided into four sections—one for persons of leisure, one for those in a hurry, one for peddlers, and one for beggars."

"Highly original," said the Bibliomaniac.

"And so cheap," added the School-Master.

"In no part of the world," said the Idiot, in response to the last comment, "do we get something for nothing. Of course this scheme would be costly, but it would increase prosperity—"

"Ha! ha!" laughed the School-Master, satirically.

"Laugh away, but you cannot gainsay my point. Our prosperity would increase, for we should not be always excavating to get at our pipes; our surface cars with a clear track would gain for us rapid transit, our truck-drivers would not be subjected to the temptations of stopping by the wayside to overturn a coupé, or to run down a pedestrian; our fine equipages would in consequence need fewer repairs; and as for the pedestrians, the beggars, if relegated to themselves, would be forced out of business as would also the street-peddlers. The men in a hurry would not be delayed by loungers, beggars, and peddlers; and the loungers would derive inestimable benefit from the arrangement in the saving of wear and tear on their clothes and minds by contact with the busy world."

"It would be delightful," acceded the School-Master, "particularly on Sundays, when they were all loungers."

"Yes," replied the Idiot. "It would be delightful then, especially in summer, when covered with an awning to shield promenaders from the sun."

Mr. Pedagog sighed, and the Bibliomaniac, wearily declining a second cup of coffee, left the table with the Doctor, earnestly discussing with that worthy gentleman the causes of weakmindedness.

VIII

"There's a friend of mine up near Riverdale," said the Idiot, as he unfolded his napkin and let his bill flutter from it to the floor, "who's tried to make a name for himself in literature."

"What's his name?" asked the Bibliomaniac, interested at once.

"That's just the trouble. He hasn't made it yet," replied the Idiot. "He hasn't succeeded in his courtship of the Muse, and beyond himself and a few friends his name is utterly unknown."

"What work has he tried?" queried the School-Master, pouring unadmonished two portions of skimmed milk over his oatmeal.

"A little of everything. First he wrote a novel. It had an immense circulation, and he only lost $300 on it. All of his friends took a copy—I've got one that he gave me—and I believe two hundred newspapers were fortunate enough to secure the book for review. His father bought two, and tried to obtain the balance of the edition, but didn't have enough money. That was gratifying, but gratification is more apt to deplete than to strengthen a bank account."

"I had not expected so extraordinarily wise an observation from one so unusually unwise," said the School-Master, coldly.

"Thank you," returned the Idiot. "But I think your remark is rather contradictory. You would naturally expect wise observations from the unusually unwise; that is, if your teaching that the expression 'unusually unwise' is but another form of the expression 'usually wise' is correct. But, as I was saying, when the genial instructor of youth interrupted me with his flattery," continued the Idiot, "gratification is gratifying but not filling, so my friend concluded that he had better give up novel-writing and try jokes. He kept at that a year, and managed to clear his postage-stamps. His jokes were good, but too classic for the tastes of the editors. Editors are peculiar. They have no respect for age—particularly in the matter of jests. Some of my friend's jokes had seemed good enough for Plutarch to print when he had a publisher at his mercy, but they didn't seem to suit the high and mighty products of this age who sit in judgment on such things in the comic-paper offices. So he gave up jokes."

"Does he still know you?" asked the landlady.

"Yes, madame," observed the Idiot.

"Then he hasn't given up all jokes," she retorted, with fine scorn.

"Tee-he-hee!" laughed the School-Master. "Pretty good, Mrs. Smithers—pretty good."

"Yes," said the Idiot. "That is good, and, by Jove! it differs from your butter, Mrs. Smithers, because it's entirely fresh. It's good enough to print, and I don't think the butter is."

"What did your friend do next?" asked Mr. Whitechoker.

"He was employed by a funeral director in Philadelphia to write obituary verses for memorial cards."

"And was he successful?"

"For a time; but he lost his position because of an error made by a careless compositor in a marble-yard. He had written,

"'Here lies the hero of a hundred fights—
　Approximated he a perfect man;
He fought for country and his country's rights,
　And in the hottest battles led the van.'"

"Fine in sentiment and in execution!" observed Mr. Whitechoker.

"Truly so," returned the Idiot. "But when the compositor in the marble-yard got it engraved on the monument, my friend was away, and when the army post that was to pay the bill received the monument, the quatrain read,

"'Here lies the hero of a hundred flights—
　Approximated he a perfect one;
He fought his country and his country's rights,
　And in the hottest battles led the run.'"

"Awful!" ejaculated the Minister.

"Dreadful!" said the landlady, forgetting to be sarcastic.

"What happened?" asked the School-Master.

"He was bounced, of course, without a cent of pay, and the company failed the next week, so he couldn't make anything by suing for what they owed him."

"Mighty hard luck," said the Bibliomaniac.

"Very; but there was one bright side to the case," observed the Idiot. "He managed to sell both versions of the quatrain afterwards for five dollars. He sold the original one to a religious weekly for a dollar, and got four dollars for the other one from a comic paper. Then he wrote an anecdote about the whole thing for a Sunday newspaper, and got three dollars more out of it."

"And what is your friend doing now?" asked the Doctor.

"Oh, he's making a mint of money now, but no name."

"In literature?"

"Yes. He writes advertisements on salary," returned the Idiot. "He is writing now a recommendation of tooth-powder in Indian dialect."

"Why didn't he try writing an epic?" said the Bibliomaniac.

"Because," replied the Idiot, "the one aim of his life has been to be original, and he couldn't reconcile that with epic poetry."

At which remark the landlady stooped over, and recovering the Idiot's bill from under the table, called the maid, and ostentatiously requested her to hand it to the Idiot. He, taking a cigarette from his pocket, thanked the maid for the attention, and rolling the slip into a taper, thoughtfully stuck one end of it into the alcohol light under the coffee-pot, and lighting the cigarette with it, walked nonchalantly from the room.

IX

"I'VE just been reading a book," began the Idiot.

"I thought you looked rather pale," said the School-Master.

"Yes," returned the Idiot, cheerfully, "it made me feel pale. It was about the pleasures of country life; and when I contrasted rural blessedness as it was there depicted with urban life as we live it, I felt as if my youth were being thrown away. I still feel as if I were wasting my sweetness on the desert air."

"Why don't you move?" queried the Bibliomaniac, suggestively.

"If I were purely selfish I should do so at once, but I am, like my good friend Mr. Whitechoker, a slave to duty. I deem it my duty to stay here to keep the School-Master fully informed in the various branches of knowledge which are day by day opened up, many of which seem to be so far beyond the reach of one of his conservative habits; to assist Mr. Whitechoker in his crusades against vice at this table and elsewhere; to give the Bibliomaniac the benefit of my advice in regard to those precious little tomes he no longer buys—to make life worth the living for all of you, to say nothing of enabling Mrs. Smithers to keep up the extraordinarily high standard of this house by means of the hard-earned stipend I pay to her every Monday morning."

"Every Monday?" queried the School-Master.

"Every Monday," returned the Idiot. "That is, of course, every Monday that I pay. The things one gets to eat in the country, the air one breathes, the utter freedom from restraint, the thousand and more things one enjoys in the suburbs that are not attainable here—it is these that make my heart yearn for the open."

"Well, it's all rot," said the School-Master, impatiently. "Country life is ideal only in books. Books do not tell of running for trains through blinding snowstorms; writers do not expatiate on the delights of waking on cold winter nights and finding your piano and parlor furniture afloat because of bursted pipes, with the plumber, like Sheridan at Winchester, twenty miles away. They are dumb on the subject of the ecstasy one feels when pushing a twenty-pound lawn-mower up and down a weed patch at the end of a wearisome hot summer's day. They are silent—"

"Don't get excited, Mr. Pedagog, please," interrupted the Idiot. "I am not contemplating leaving you and Mrs. Smithers, but I do pine for a little garden of my own, where I could raise an occasional can of

"'A HIND-QUARTER OF LAMB GAMBOLLING ABOUT ITS NATIVE HEATH'" tomatoes. I dream sometimes of getting milk fresh from the pump, instead of twenty-four hours after it has been drawn, as we do here. In my musings it seems to me to be almost idyllic to have known a spring chicken in his infancy; to have watched a hind-quarter of lamb gambolling about its native heath before its muscles became adamant, and before chopped-up celery tops steeped in vinegar were poured upon it in the hope of hypnotizing boarders into the belief that spring lamb and mint-sauce lay before them. What care I how hard it is to rise every morning before six in winter to thaw out the boiler, so long as the night coming finds me seated in the genial glow of the gas log! What man is he that would complain of having to bale out his cellar every week, if, on the other hand, that cellar gains thereby a fertility that keeps its floor sheeny, soft, and green—an interior tennis-court—from spring to spring, causing the gladsome click of the lawn-mower to be heard within its walls all through the still watches of the winter day? I tell you, sir, it is the life to lead, that of our rural brother. I do not believe that in this whole vast city there is a cellar like that—an

"'A LITTLE GARDEN OF MY OWN, WHERE I COULD RAISE AN OCCASIONAL CAN OF TOMATOES'"

in-door garden-patch, as it were. Do you happen to recall one?"

"No," returned the Doctor; "and it is a good thing there isn't. There is enough sickness in the world without bringing any of your *rus* ideas *in urbe*. I've lived in the country, sir, and I assure you it is not what

"'THE GLADSOME CLICK OF THE LAWN-MOWER'"

it is written up to be. Country life is misery, melancholy, and malaria."

"You must have struck a profitable section, Doctor," returned the Idiot, taking possession of three steaming buckwheat cakes to the dismay of Mr. Whitechoker, who was about to reach out for them himself. "And I should have supposed that your good business sense would have restrained you from leaving."

"Then the countryman is poor—always poor," continued the Doctor, ignoring the Idiot's sarcastic comments.

"Ah! that accounts for it," observed the Idiot. "I see why you did not stay; for what shall it profit a man to save a patient if practice, like virtue, is to be its own reward?"

"Your suggestion, sir," retorted the Doctor, "betrays an unhealthy frame of mind."

"That's all right, Doctor," returned the Idiot; "but please do not diagnose the case any further. I can't afford an expert opinion as to my mental condition. But to return to our subject: you two gentlemen appear to have had unhappy experiences in country life—quite different from those of a friend of mine who owns a farm. He doesn't have to run for trains; he is independent of plumbers, because the only pipes in his house are for smoking purposes. The farm produces corn enough to keep his family supplied all the year round and to sell a balance at a profit. Oats and wheat are harvested to an extent which keeps the cattle and declares dividends besides. He never suffers from the cold or heat. He is never afraid of losing his house or barns by fire, because the whole fire department of the neighboring village is, to a man, in love with the housekeeper's daughter, and is always on hand in force. The chickens are the envy and pride of the county, and there are so many of them that they have to take turns in going to roost. The pigs are the most intelligent of their kind, and are so happy they never grunt. In fact, everything is lovely and cheap, the only thing that hangs high being the goose."

"Quite an ideal, no doubt," put in the School-Master, scornfully. "I suppose his is one of those model farms with steam-pipes under the walks to melt the snow in winter, and of course there is a vein of coal growing right up into his furnace ready to be lit."

"Yes," observed the Bibliomaniac; "and no doubt the chickens lay eggs in every style—poached, fried, scrambled, and boiled.

The weeds in the garden grow so fast, I suppose, that they pull themselves up by the roots; and if there is anything left undone at the end of the day I presume tramps in dress suits, and courtly in manner, spring out of the ground and finish up for him without charge."

"I'll bet he's not on good terms with his neighbors if he has everything you speak of in such perfection. These farmers get frightfully jealous of each other," asserted the Doctor, with a positiveness that seemed to be born of experience.

"He never quarrelled with one of them in his life," returned the Idiot. "He doesn't know them well enough to quarrel with them; in fact, I doubt if he ever sees them at all. He's very exclusive."

"Of course he is a born farmer to get everything the way he has it," suggested Mrs. Smithers.

"No, he isn't. He's a broker," said the Idiot, "and a very successful one. I see him on the street every day."

"Does he employ a man to run the farm?" asked the Clergyman.

"No," returned the Idiot, "he has too

much sense and too few dollars to do any such foolish thing as that."

"It must be one of those self-winding stock farms," put in the School-Master, scornfully. "But I don't see how he can be a successful broker and make money off his farm at the same time. Your statements do not agree, either. You said he never had to run for trains."

"Well, he never has," returned the Idiot, calmly. "He never goes near his farm. He doesn't have to. It's leased to the husband of the house-keeper whose daughter has a crush on the fire department. He takes his pay in produce, and gets more than if he took it in cash on the basis of the New York vegetable market."

"Then you have got us into an argument about country life that ends—" began the School-Master, indignantly.

"That ends where it leaves off," retorted the Idiot, departing with a smile on his lips.

"He's an Idiot from Idaho," asserted the Bibliomaniac.

"Yes; but I'm afraid idiocy is contagious," observed the Doctor, with a grin and sidelong glance at the School-Master.

X

"Good-morning, gentlemen," said the Idiot, as he seated himself at the breakfast-table and glanced over his mail.

"Good-morning yourself," returned the Poet. "You have an unusually large number of letters this morning. All checks, I hope?"

"Yes," replied the Idiot. "All checks of one kind or another. Mostly checks on ambition—otherwise, rejections from my friends the editors."

"You don't mean to say that you write for the papers?" put in the School-Master, with an incredulous smile.

"I try to," returned the Idiot, meekly. "If the papers don't take 'em, I find them useful in curing my genial friend who imbibes of insomnia."

"What do you write—advertisements?" queried the Bibliomaniac.

"No. Advertisement writing is an art to which I dare not aspire. It's too great a tax on the brain," replied the Idiot.

"Tax on what?" asked the Doctor. He was going to squelch the Idiot.

"The brain," returned the latter, not ready to be squelched. "It's a little thing people use to think with, Doctor. I'd advise you to get one." Then he added, "I write poems and foreign letters mostly."

"I did not know that you had ever been abroad," said the Clergyman.

"I never have," returned the Idiot.

"Then how, may I ask," said Mr. White-

"'YOU DON'T MEAN TO SAY THAT YOU WRITE FOR THE PAPERS?'"

choker, severely, "how can you write foreign letters?"

"With my stub pen, of course," replied the Idiot. "How did you suppose—with an oyster-knife?"

The Clergyman sighed.

"I should like to hear some of your poems," said the Poet.

"Very well," returned the Idiot. "Here's one that has just returned from the *Bengal Monthly*. It's about a writer who died some years ago. Shakespeare's his name. You've heard of Shakespeare, haven't you, Mr. Pedagog?" he added.

Then, as there was no answer, he read the verse, which was as follows:

SETTLED.

Yes! Shakespeare wrote the plays—'tis clear to me.
Lord Bacon's claim's condemned before the bar.
He'd not have penned, "what fools these mortals
 be!"
But—more correct—"what fools these mortals
 are!"

"That's not bad," said the Poet.

"Thanks," returned the Idiot. "I wish you were an editor. I wrote that last spring, and it has been coming back to me at the rate of once a week ever since."

"It is too short," said the Bibliomaniac.

"It's an epigram," said the Idiot. "How many yards long do you think epigrams should be?"

The Bibliomaniac scorned to reply.

"I agree with the Bibliomaniac," said the School-Master. "It is too short. People want greater quantity."

"Well, here is quantity for you," said the Idiot. "Quantity as she is not wanted by nine comic papers I wot of. This poem is called:

"'THE TURNING OF THE WORM.

"'How hard my fate perhaps you'll gather in,
  My dearest reader, when I tell you that
I entered into this fair world a twin—
  The one was spare enough, the other fat.

"'I was, of course, the lean one of the two,
  The homelier as well, and consequently
In ecstasy o'er Jim my parents flew,
  And good of me was spoken accident'ly.

"'As boys we went to school, and Jim, of course,
  Was e'er his teacher's favorite, and ranked
Among the lads renowned for moral force,
  Whilst I was every day right soundly spanked.

"'Jim had an angel face, but there he stopped.
   I never knew a lad who'd sin so oft
And look so like a branch of heaven lopped
   From off the parent trunk that grows aloft.

"'I seemed an imp—indeed 'twas often said
   That I resembled much Beelzebub.
My face was freckled and my hair was red—
   The kind of looking boy that men call scrub.

"'Kind deeds, however, were my constant thought;
   In everything I did the best I could;
I said my prayers thrice daily, and I sought
   In all my ways to do the right and good.

"'On Saturdays I'd do my Monday's sums,
   While Jim would spend the day in search of fun;
He'd sneak away and steal the neighbor's plums,
   And, strange to say, to earth was never run.

"'Whilst I, when study-time was haply through,
   Would seek my brother in the neighbor's orchard;
Would find the neighbor there with anger blue,
   And as the thieving culprit would be tortured.

"'The sums I'd done he'd steal, this lad forsaken,
   Then change my work, so that a paltry four
Would be my mark, whilst he had overtaken
   The maximum and all the prizes bore.

"'In later years we loved the self-same maid;
 We sent her little presents, sweets, bouquets,
For which, alas! 'twas I that always paid;
 And Jim the maid now honors and obeys.

"'We entered politics—in different roles,
 And for a minor office each did run.
'Twas I was left—left badly at the polls,
 Because of fishy things that Jim had done.

"'When Jim went into business and failed,
 I signed his notes and freed him from the strife.
Which bankruptcy and ruin hath entailed
 On them that lead a queer financial life.

"'Then, penniless, I learned that Jim had set
 Aside before his failure—hard to tell!—
A half a million dollars on his pet—
 His Mrs. Jim—the former lovely Nell.

"'That wearied me of Jim. It may be right
 For one to bear another's cross, but I
Quite fail to see it in its proper light,
 If that's the rule man should be guided by.

"'And since a fate perverse has had the wit
 To mix us up so that the one's deserts
Upon the shoulders of the other sit,
 No matter how the other one it hurts,

"'I am resolved to take some mortal's life;
   Just when, or where, or how, I do not reck,
So long as law will end this horrid strife
   And twist my dear twin brother's sinful neck.'"

"There," said the Idiot, putting down the manuscript. "How's that?"

"I don't like it," said Mr. Whitechoker. "It is immoral and vindictive. You should accept the hardships of life, no matter how unjust. The conclusion of your poem horrifies me, sir. I—"

"Have you tried your hand at dialect poetry?" asked the Doctor.

"Yes; once," said the Idiot. "I sent it to the *Great Western Weekly*. Oh yes. Here it is. Sent back with thanks. It's an octette written in cigar-box dialect."

"In wh-a-at?" asked the Poet.

"Cigar-box dialect. Here it is:

"'O Manuel garcia alonzo,
   Colorado especial H. Clay,
Invincible flora alphonzo,
   Cigarette panatella el rey,
Victoria reina selectas—
   O twofer madura grandé—
O conchas oscuro perfectas,
   You drive all my sorrows away.'"

"Ingenious, but vicious," said the School-Master, who does not smoke.

"Again thanks. How is this for a sonnet?" said the Idiot:

"'When to the sessions of sweet silent thought
I summon up remembrance of things past,
I sigh the lack of many a thing I sought,
And with old woes new wail my dear time's waste:
Then can I drown an eye, unused to flow,
For precious friends hid in death's dateless night,
And weep afresh love's long since cancel'd woe,
And moan the expense of many a vanish'd sight:
Then can I grieve at grievances foregone,
And heavily from woe to woe tell o'er
The sad account of fore-bemoaned moan,
Which I now pay as if not paid before.
But if the while I think of thee, dear friend!
All losses are restored and sorrows end.'"

"It is bosh!" said the School-Master.

The Poet smiled quietly.

"Perfect bosh!" repeated the School-Master. "And only shows how in weak hands so beautiful a thing as the sonnet can be made ridiculous."

"What's wrong with it?" asked the Idiot.

"It doesn't contain any thought—or if it

does, no one can tell what the thought is. Your rhymes are atrocious. Your phraseology is ridiculous. The whole thing is bad. You'll never get anybody to print it."

"I do not intend to try," said the Idiot, meekly.

"You are wise," said the School-Master, "to take my advice for once."

"No, it is not your advice that restrains me," said the Idiot, dryly. "It is the fact that this sonnet has already been printed."

"In the name of Letters, where?" cried the School-Master.

"In the collected works of William Shakespeare," replied the Idiot, quietly.

The Poet laughed; Mrs. Smithers's eyes filled with tears; and the School-Master for once had absolutely nothing to say.

XI

"Do you believe, Mr. Whitechoker," said the Idiot, taking his place at the table, and holding his plate up to the light, apparently to see whether or not it was immaculate, whereat the landlady sniffed comtemptuously—"do you believe that the love of money is the root of all evil?"

"I have always been of that impression," returned Mr. Whitechoker, pleasantly. "In fact, I am sure of it," he added. "There is no evil thing in this world, sir, that cannot be traced back to a point where greed is found to be its main-spring and the source of its strength."

"Then how do you reconcile this with the scriptural story of the forbidden fruit? Do you think the apples referred to were figures of speech, the true import of which was that Adam and Eve had their eyes on the original surplus?"

"Well, of course, there you begin to—ah—you seem to me to be going back to the—er—the—ah—"

"Original root of all evil," prompted the Idiot, calmly.

"Precisely," returned Mr. Whitechoker, with a sigh of relief. "Mrs. Smithers, I think I'll have a dash of hot water in my coffee this morning." Then, with a nervous glance towards the Idiot, he added, addressing the Bibliomaniac, "I think it looks like rain."

"Referring to the coffee, Mr. Whitechoker?" queried the Idiot, not disposed to let go of his victim quite so easily.

"Ah—I don't quite follow you," replied the Minister, with some annoyance.

"You said something looked like rain, and I asked you if the thing you referred to was the coffee, for I was disposed to agree with you," said the Idiot.

"I am sure," put in Mrs. Smithers, "that a gentleman of Mr. Whitechoker's refinement would not make any such insinuation, sir. He is not the man to quarrel with what is set before him."

"I ask your pardon, madame," returned

the Idiot, politely. "I hope that I am not the man to quarrel with my food, either. Indeed, I make it a rule to avoid unpleasantness of all sorts, particularly with the weak, under which category we find your coffee. I simply wish to know to what Mr. Whitechoker refers when he says 'it looks like rain.'"

"I mean, of course," said the Minister, with as much calmness as he could command—and that was not much—"I mean the day. The day looks as if it might be rainy."

"Any one with a modicum of brain knows what you meant, Mr. Whitechoker," volunteered the School-Master.

"Certainly," observed the Idiot, scraping the butter from his toast; "but to those who have more than a modicum of brains my reverend friend's remark was not entirely clear. If I am talking of cotton, and a gentleman chooses to state that it looks like snow, I know exactly what he means. He doesn't mean that the day looks like snow, however; he refers to the cotton. Mr. Whitechoker, talking about coffee, chooses to state that it looks like rain, which it undoubtedly does. I, realizing that, as Mrs. Smithers says, it is not the gentleman's habit to attack too violently the food which is set before him, manifest some surprise, and, giving the gentleman the benefit of the doubt, afford him an opportunity to set himself right."

"Change the subject," said the Bibliomaniac, curtly.

"With pleasure," answered the Idiot, filling his glass with cream. "We'll change the subject, or the object, or anything you choose. We'll have another breakfast, or another variety of biscuits *frappé*—anything, in short, to keep peace at the table. Tell me, Mr. Pedagog," he added, "is the use of the word 'it' in the sentence 'it looks like rain,' perfectly correct?"

"I don't know why it is not," returned the School-Master, uneasily. He was not at all desirous of parleying with the Idiot.

"And is it correct to suppose that 'it' refers to the day—is the day supposed to look like rain?—or do we simply use 'it' to express a condition which confronts us?"

"It refers to the latter, of course."

"Then the full text of Mr. Whitechoker's

remark is, I suppose, that 'the rainy condition of the atmosphere which confronts us looks like rain?'"

"Oh, I suppose so," sighed the School-Master, wearily.

"Rather an unnecessary sort of statement that!" continued the Idiot. "It's something like asserting that a man looks like himself, or, as in the case of a child's primer—

"'See the cat?'

"'Yes, I see the cat.'

"'What is the cat?'

"'The cat is a cat. Scat cat!'"

At this even Mrs. Smithers smiled.

"I don't agree with Mr. Pedagog," put in the Bibliomaniac, after a pause.

Here the School-Master shook his head warningly at the Bibliomaniac, as if to indicate that he was not in good form.

"So I observe," remarked the Idiot. "You have upset him completely. See how Mr. Pedagog trembles?" he added, addressing the genial gentleman who occasionally imbibed.

"I don't mean that way," sneered the Bibliomaniac, bound to set Mr. Whitechoker straight. "I mean that the word 'it,' as employed in that sentence, stands for day. The day looks like rain."

"Did you ever see a day?" queried the Idiot.

"Certainly I have," returned the Bibliomaniac.

"What does it look like?" was the calmly put question.

The Bibliomaniac's impatience was here almost too great for safety, and the manner in which his face colored aroused considerable interest in the breast of the Doctor, who was a good deal of a specialist in apoplexy.

"Was it a whole day you saw, or only a half-day?" persisted the Idiot.

"You may think you are very funny," retorted the Bibliomaniac. "I think you are—"

"Now don't get angry," returned the Idiot. "There are two or three things I do not know, and I am anxious to learn. I'd like to know how a day looks to one to whom it is a visible object. If it is visible, is it tangible? and if so, how does it feel? I never felt a day myself."

"The visible is always tangible," asserted the School-Master, recklessly.

"How about a red-hot stove, or manifest indignation, or a view from a mountain-top, or, as in the case of the young man in the novel who 'suddenly waked,' and, 'looking anxiously about him, saw no one?'" returned the Idiot, imperturbably.

"Tut!" ejaculated the Bibliomaniac. "If I had brains like yours, I'd blow them out."

"Yes, I think you would," observed the Idiot, folding up his napkin. "You're just the man to do a thing like that. I believe you'd blow out the gas in your bedroom if there wasn't a sign over it requesting you not to." And filling his match-box from the landlady's mantel supply, the Idiot hurried from the room, and soon after left the house.

XII

"IF my father hadn't met with reverses—" the Idiot began.

"Did you really have a father?" interrupted the School-Master. "I thought you were one of these self-made Idiots. How terrible it must be for a man to think that he is responsible for you!"

"Yes," rejoined the Idiot; "my father finds it rather hard to stand up under his responsibility for me; but he is a brave old gentleman, and he manages to bear the burden very well with the aid of my mother—for I have a mother, too, Mr. Pedagog. A womanly mother she is, too, with all the natural follies, such as fondness for and belief in her boy. Why, it would soften your heart to see how she looks on me. She thinks I am the most everlastingly brilliant man she ever knew—excepting father, of course, who has always been a hero of heroes in her eyes, because he never rails at misfortune, never spoke an unkind word to her in his life, and just lives gently along waiting for the end of all things."

"Do you think it is right in you to deceive your mother in this way—making her think you a young Napoleon of intellect when you know you are an Idiot?" observed the Bibliomaniac, with a twinkle in his eye.

"Why certainly I do," returned the Idiot, calmly. "It's my place to make the old folks happy if I can; and if thinking me nineteen different kinds of a genius is going to fill my mother's heart with happiness, I'm going to let her think it. What's the use of destroying other people's idols even if we do know them to be hollow mockeries? Do you think you do a praiseworthy act, for instance, when you kick over the heathen's stone gods and leave him without any at all? You may not have noticed it, but I have—that it is easier to pull down an idol than it is to rear an ideal. I have had idols shattered myself, and I haven't found that the pedestals they used to occupy have been rented since. They are there yet and empty—standing as monuments to what once seemed good to me—and I'm no happier nor no better for being disillusioned. So it is with my mother. I let her go on and think me perfect. It does her good, and it does me good because it makes me try to live up to that idea of hers as to what I am. If she had the same opinion of me that we all have she'd be the most miserable woman in the world."

"We don't all think so badly of you," said the Doctor, rather softened by the Idiot's remarks.

"No," put in the Bibliomaniac. "You are all right. You breathe normally, and you have nice blue eyes. You are graceful and pleasant to look upon, and if you'd been born dumb we'd esteem you very highly. It is only your manners and your theories that we don't like; but even in these we are disposed to believe that you are a well-meaning child."

"That is precisely the way to put it," assented the School-Master. "You are harmless even when most annoying. For my own part, I think the most objectionable feature about you is that you suffer from that unfortunately not uncommon malady, extreme youth. You are young for your age, and if you only wouldn't talk, I think we should get on famously together."

"You overwhelm me with your compliments," said the Idiot. "I am sorry I am so young, but I cannot be brought to believe that that is my own fault. One must live to attain age, and how the deuce can one live when one boards?"

As no one ventured to reply to this question, the force of which very evidently, however, was fully appreciated by Mrs. Smithers, the Idiot continued:

"Youth is thrust upon us in our infancy, and must be endured until such a time as Fate permits us to account ourselves cured. It swoops down upon us when we have neither the strength nor the brains to resent it. Of course there are some superior persons in this world who never were young. Mr. Pedagog, I doubt not, was ushered into this world with all three sets of teeth cut, and not wailing as most infants are, but discussing the most abstruse philosophical problems. His fairy stories were told him, if ever, in words of ten syllables; and his father's first remark to him was doubtless an inquiry as to his opinion on the subject of Latin and Greek in our colleges. It's all right to be this kind of a baby if you like that sort of thing. For my part, I rejoice to think that there was once a day when I thought my father a mean-spirited assassin, because he wouldn't tie a string to the moon and let me make it rise and set as suited my sweet will. Babies of Mr. Pedagog's sort are fortunately like angels' visits, few and far between. In spite of his stand in the matter, though, I can't help thinking there was a great deal of truth in a rhyme a friend of mine got off on Youth. It fits the case. He said:

" 'Youth is a state of being we attain
  In early years; to some 'tis but a crime—
  And, like the mumps, most agèd men complain,
  It can't be caught, alas! a second time.' "

"Your rhymes are interesting, and your reasoning, as usual, is faulty," said the School-Master. "I passed a very pleasant childhood, though it was a childhood devoted, as you have insinuated, to serious rather than to flippant pursuits. I wasn't particularly fond of tag and hide-and-seek, nor do I think that even as an infant I ever cried for the moon."

"It would have expanded your chest if you had, Mr. Pedagog," observed the Idiot, quietly.

"So it would, but I never found myself short-winded, sir," retorted the School-Master, with some acerbity.

"That is evident; but go on," said the Idiot. "You never passed a childish youth nor a youthful childhood, and therefore what?"

"Therefore, in my present condition, I am normally contented. I have no youthful follies to look back upon, no indiscretions to regret; I never knowingly told a lie, and—"

"All of which proves that you never were young," put in the Idiot; "and you will excuse me if I say it, but my father is the model for me rather than so exalted a personage as yourself. He is still young, though turned seventy, and I don't believe on his own account there ever was a boy who played hookey more, who prevaricated oftener, who purloined others' fruits with greater frequency than he. He was guilty of every crime in the calendar of youth; and if there is one thing that delights him more than another, it is to sit on a winter's night before the crackling log and tell us yarns about his youthful follies and his boyhood indiscretions."

"But is he normally a happy man?" queried the School-Master.

"No."

"Ah!"

"No. He's an *ab*normally happy man, because he's got his follies and indiscretions to look back upon and not forward to."

"Ahem!" said Mrs. Smithers.

"Dear me!" ejaculated Mr. Whitechoker.

Mr. Pedagog said nothing, and the breakfast-room was soon deserted.

XIII

THERE was an air of suppressed excitement about Mrs. Smithers and Mr. Pedagog as they sat down to breakfast. Something had happened, but just what that something was no one as yet knew, although the genial old gentleman had a sort of notion as to what it was.

"Pedagog has been good-natured enough for an engaged man for nearly a week now," he whispered to the Idiot, who had asked him what he supposed was up, "and I have a half idea that Mrs. S. has at last brought him to the point of proposing."

"It's the other way, I imagine," returned the Idiot.

"You don't really think she has rejected him, do you?" queried the genial old gentleman.

"Oh, no; not by a great deal. I mean

that I think it very likely that he has brought her to the point. This is leap-year, you know," said the Idiot.

"Well, if I were a betting man, which I haven't been since night before last, I'd lay you a wager that they're engaged," said the old gentleman.

"I'm glad you've given up betting," rejoined the Idiot, "because I'm sure I'd take the bet if you offered it—and then I believe I'd lose."

"We are to have Philadelphia spring chickens this morning, gentlemen," said Mrs. Smithers, beaming upon all at the table. "It's a special treat."

"Which we all appreciate, my dear Mrs. Smithers," observed the Idiot, with a courteous bow to his landlady. "And, by the way, why is it that Philadelphia spring chickens do not appear until autumn, do you suppose? Is it because Philadelphia spring doesn't get around until it is autumn everywhere else?"

"No, I think not," said the Doctor. "I think it is because Philadelphia spring chickens are not sufficiently hardened to be able to stand the strain of exportation much before September, or else Philadelphia people do not get so sated with such delicacies as to permit any of the crop to go into other than Philadelphia markets before that period. For my part, I simply love them."

"So do I," said the Idiot; "and if Mrs. Smithers will pardon me for expressing a preference for any especial part of the *pièce de résistance,* I will state to her that if, in helping me, she will give me two drumsticks, a pair of second joints, and plenty of the white meat, I shall be very happy."

"You ought to have said so yesterday," said the School-Master, with a surprisingly genial laugh. "Then Mrs. Smithers could have prepared an individual chicken for you."

"That would be too much," returned the Idiot, "and I should really hesitate to eat too much spring chicken. I never did it in my life, and don't know what the effect would be. Would it be harmful, Doctor?"

"I really do not know how it would be," answered the Doctor. "In all my wide experience I have never found a case of the kind."

"It's very rarely that one gets too much

spring chicken," said Mr. Whitechoker. "I haven't had any experience with patients, as my friend the Doctor has; but I have lived in many boarding-houses, and I have never yet known of any one even getting enough."

"Well, perhaps we shall have all we want this morning," said Mrs. Smithers. "I hope so, at any rate, for I wish this day to be a memorable one in our house. Mr. Pedagog has something to tell you. John, will you announce it now?"

"Did you hear that?" whispered the Idiot. "She called him 'John.'"

"Yes," said the genial old gentleman. "I didn't know Pedagog had a first name before."

"Certainly, my dear—that is, my very dear Mrs. Smithers," stammered the School-Master, getting red in the face. "The fact is, gentlemen—ahem!—I—er—we—er—that is, of course—er—Mrs. Smithers has er—ahem! —Mrs. Smithers has asked me to be her— I—er—I should say I have asked Mrs. Smithers to be my husb—my wife, and—er —she—"

"Hoorah!" cried the Idiot, jumping up from the table and grasping Mr. Pedagog by the hand. "Hoorah! You've got in ahead of us, old man, but we are just as glad when we think of your good-fortune. Your gain may be our loss—but what of that where the happiness of our dear landlady is at stake?"

Mrs. Smithers glanced coyly at the Idiot and smiled.

"Thank you," said the School-Master.

"You are welcome," said the Idiot. "Mrs. Smithers, you will also permit me to felicitate you upon this happy event. I, who have so often differed with Mr. Pedagog upon matters of human knowledge, am forced to admit that upon this occasion he has shown such eminently good sense that you are fortunate, indeed, to have won him."

"Again I thank you," said the School-Master. "You are a very sensible person yourself, my dear Idiot; perhaps my failure to appreciate you at times in the past has been due to your brilliant qualities, which have so dazzled me that I have been unable to see you as you really are."

"Here are the chickens," said Mrs. Smithers.

"Ah!" ejaculated the Idiot. "What lucky fellows we are, to be sure! I hope,

Mrs. Smithers, now that Mr. Pedagog has cut us all out, you will at least be a sister to the rest of us, and let us live at home."

"There is to be no change," said Mrs. Smithers—" at least, I hope not, except that Mr. Pedagog will take a more active part in the management of our home."

"I don't envy him that," said the Idiot. "We shall be severe critics, and it will be hard work for him to manage affairs better than you did, Mrs. Smithers."

"Mary, get me a larger cup for the Idiot's coffee," said Mrs. Smithers.

"Let's all retire from business," suggested the Idiot, after the other guests had expressed their satisfaction with the turn affairs had taken. "Let's retire from business, and change the Smithers Home for Boarders into an Educational Institution."

"For what purpose?" queried the Bibliomaniac.

"Everything is so lovely now," explained the Idiot, "that I feel as though I never wanted to leave the house again, even to win a fortune. If we turn it into a college and instruct youth, we need never go outside the front door excepting for pleasure."

"Where will the money and the instructors come from?" asked Mr. Whitechoker.

"Money? From pupils; and after we get going maybe somebody will endow us. As for instructors, I think we know enough to be instructors ourselves," replied the Idiot. "For instance: Pedagog's University. John Pedagog, President; Alonzo B. Whitechoker, Chaplain; Mrs. Smithers-Pedagog, Matron. For Professor of Belles-lettres, the Bibliomaniac, assisted by the Poet; Medical Lectures by Dr. Capsule; Chemistry taught by our genial friend who occasionally imbibes; Chair in General Information, your humble servant. Why, we would be overrun with pupils and money in less than a year."

"A very good idea," returned Mr. Pedagog. "I have often thought that a nice little school could be started here to advantage, though I must confess that I had different ideas on the subject of the instructors. You, my dear Idiot, would be a great deal more useful as a Professor Emeritus."

"H'm!" said the Idiot. "It sounds mighty well—I've no doubt I should like it. What is a Professor Emeritus, Mr. Pedagog?"

"He is a professor who is paid a salary for doing nothing."

The whole table joined in a laugh, the Idiot included.

"By Jove! Mr. Pedagog," he said, as soon as he could speak, "you are just dead right about that. That's the place of places for me. Salary and nothing to do! Oh, how I'd love it!"

The rest of the breakfast was eaten in silence. The spring chickens were too good and too plentiful to admit of much waste of time in conversation. At the conclusion of the meal the Idiot rose from the table, and, after again congratulating Mr. Pedagog and his fiancée, announced that he was going to see his employer.

"On Sunday?" queried Mrs. Smithers.

"Yes; I want him to write me a recommendation as a man who can do nothing beautifully."

"And why, pray?" asked Mr. Pedagog.

"I'm going to apply to the Trustees of Columbia College the first thing to-morrow morning for an Emeritus Professorship, for if anybody can do nothing and draw money for it gracefully I'm the man. Wall Street is too wearing on my nerves, and I'm going to leave it," he replied.

And in a moment he was gone.

"I *like* him," said Mrs. Smithers.

"So do I," said Mr. Pedagog. "He isn't half the idiot he thinks he is."

THE IDIOT

TO
WILLIAM K. OTIS

THE IDIOT

I

FOR some weeks after the happy event which transformed the popular Mrs. Smithers into the charming Mrs. John Pedagog all went well at that lady's select home for single gentlemen. It was only proper that during the honey-moon, at least, of the happy couple hostilities between the Idiot and his fellow-boarders should cease. It was expecting too much of mankind, however, to look for a continued armistice, and the morning arrived when Nature once more reasserted herself, and trouble began. Just what it was that prompted the remark no one knows, but it happened that the Idiot did say that he thought that, after all, life on a canal-boat had its advantages. Mr. Pedagog, who had come into the dining-room in a slightly irritable frame of mind, induced perhaps by Mrs.

Pedagog's insistence that as he was now part proprietor of the house he should be a little more prompt in making his contributions towards its maintenance, chose to take the remark as implying a reflection upon the way things were managed in the household.

"Humph!" he said. "I had hoped that your habit of airing your idiotic views had been put aside for once and for all."

"Very absurd hope, my dear sir," observed the Idiot. "Views that are not aired become musty. Why shouldn't I give them an atmospheric opportunity once in a while?"

"Because they are the sort of views to which suffocation is the most appropriate end," snapped the School-Master. "Any man who asserts, as you have asserted, that life on a canal-boat has its advantages, ought to go further, and prove his sincerity by living on one."

"I can't afford it," said the Idiot, meekly. "It isn't cheap by any manner of means. In the first place, you can't live happily on a canal-boat unless you can afford to keep horses. In fact, canal-boat life is a combination of the most expensive luxuries, since it combines yachting and driving with domesticity. Nevertheless, if you will put your mind on it, you will find that with a canal-boat for your home you can do a great many things that you can't do with a house."

"I decline to put my mind on a canal-boat," said Mr. Pedagog, sharply, passing his coffee back to Mrs. Pedagog for another lump of sugar, thereby contributing to that good lady's discomfiture, since before their marriage the mere fact that the coffee had been poured by her fair hand had given it all the sweetness it needed; or at least that was what the School-Master had said, and more than once at that.

"You are under no obligation to do so," the Idiot returned. "Though if I had a mind like yours I'd put it on a canal-boat and have it towed away somewhere out of sight. These other gentlemen, however, I think, will agree with me when I say that the mere fact that a canal-boat can be moved about the country, and is in no sense a fixture anywhere, shows that as a dwelling-place it is superior to a house. Take this house, for instance. This neighborhood used to be the best in town. It is still far from being the worst neighborhood in town, but it is, as it has been for several years, deteriorating. The establishment of a Turkish bath on one corner and a grocery-store on the other has taken away much of that air of refinement which characterized it when the block was devoted to residential purposes entirely. Now just suppose for a moment that this street were a canal, and that this house were a canal-boat. The canal could run down as much as it pleased, the neighborhood could deteriorate eternally, but it could not affect the value of this house as the home of refined people as long as it was possible to hitch up a team of horses to the front stoop and tow it into a better locality. I'd like to wager every man at this table that Mrs. Pedagog wouldn't take five minutes to make up her mind to tow this house up to a spot near Central Park, if it were a canal-boat and the streets were water instead of a mixture of water, sand, and Belgian blocks."

"No takers," said the Bibliomaniac.

"Tutt-tutt-tutt," ejaculated Mr. Pedagog.

"You seem to lose sight of another fact," said the Idiot, warming up to his subject. "If man had had the sense in the beginning to adopt the canal-boat system of life, and we were used to that sort of thing, it would not be so hard upon us in summer-time, when we have to live in hotels in order that we and our families may reap the benefits of a period

"THE NUISANCE OF HAVING TO PAY"

of country life. We could simply drive off to that section of the country where we desired to be. Hotels would not be needed if a man could take his house along with him into the fields, and one phase of life which has more bad than good in it would be entirely obliterated. There is nothing more disturbing to the serenity of a domestic man's mind than the artificial manner of living that prevails in most summer hotels. The nuisance of having to pay bills every Monday morning under the penalty of losing one's luggage would be obviated, and all the comforts of home would be directly within reach. The trouble incident upon getting the trunks packed and the children ready for a long day's journey by rail, and the fatigue arising from such a journey, would be reduced to a minimum. The troubles attendant upon going into a far country, and leaving one's house in the sole charge of a lot of servants for a month or two every year, would be done away with entirely; and if at any time it became necessary to discharge one of these servants, she could be put off the boat in an instant, and then the boat could be pushed out into the middle of the canal, so that the discharged domestic could not possibly get aboard again and take her revenge by smashing your crockery and fixtures. That is one of the worst features of living in a stationary house. You are entirely at the mercy of vindictive servants. They know precisely where you live, and you cannot escape them. They can come back when there is no man around, and raise several varieties of Ned with your wife and children. With a movable house, such as the canal-boat would be, you could always go off and leave your family in perfect safety."

"How about safety in a storm?" asked the Bibliomaniac.

"Safety in a storm?" echoed the Idiot. "That seems an absurd sort of a question to one who knows anything about canal-boats. I, for one, never heard of a canal-boat being seriously damaged in a storm as long as it was anchored in the canal proper. It certainly isn't any more dangerous to be in a canal-boat in a storm than it is to be in a house that offers resistance to the winds, and is shaken from roof to cellar at every blast. More houses have been blown from their foundations than canal-boats sunk, provided ordinary care has been taken to protect them."

"SHE COULD NOT POSSIBLY GET ABOARD AGAIN"

"And you think the canal-boat would be healthy?" asked the Doctor. "How about dampness and all that?"

"That is a professional question," returned the Idiot, "which I think you could answer better than I. I don't see why a canal-boat shouldn't be healthy, however. The dampness would not amount to very much. It would be outside of one's dwelling, and not within it, as is the case with so many houses. A canal-boat having no cellar could not have a damp one, and if by some untoward circumstance it should spring a leak, the water could be pumped out at once and the leak plugged up. However this might be, I'll offer another wager to this board on that point, and that is that more people die in houses than on canal-boats."

"We'd rather give you our money right out," retorted the Doctor.

"Thank you," said the Idiot. "But I don't need money. I don't like money. Money is responsible for more extravagance than any other commodity in existence. Besides, it and I are not intimate enough to get along very well together, and when I have any I immediately do my level best to rid myself of it. But to return to our canal-boat. I note a look of disapproval in Mr. Whitechoker's eyes. He doesn't seem to think any more of my scheme than do the rest of you—which I regret, since I believe that he would be the gainer if land edifices were supplanted by the canal system as proposed by myself. Take church on a rainy morning, for instance. A great many people stay at home from church on rainy mornings just because they do not want to venture out in the wet. Suppose we all lived in canal-boats? Would not people be deprived of this flimsy pretext for staying at home if their homes could be towed up to the church door? Or, better yet, granting that the churches followed out the same plan, and were themselves constructed like canal-boats, how easy it would be for the sexton to drive the church around the town and collect the absentees. In the same manner it would be glorious for men like ourselves, who have to go to their daily toil. For a consideration, Mrs. Pedagog could have us driven to our various places of business every morning, returning for us in the evening. Think how fine it would be for me, for instance, instead of having to come home every night in an overcrowded elevated train or on a cable-car, to have the office-boy come and announce, 'Mrs. Pedagog's Select Home for Gentlemen is at the door, Mr. Idiot.' I could step right out of my office into my charming little bedroom up in the bow, and the time usually expended on the cars could be devoted to dressing for tea. Then we could stop in at the court-house for our legal friend; and as for Doctor Capsule, wouldn't he revel in driving this boarding-house about town on his daily rounds among his patients?"

"What would become of my office hours?" asked the Doctor. "If this house were whirling giddily all about the city from morning until night, I don't know what would become of my office patients."

"They might die a little sooner or live a little longer, that is all," said the Idiot. "If they weren't able to find the house at all, however, I think it would be better for us, for much as I admire you, Doctor, I think your office hours are a nuisance to the rest of us. I had to elbow my way out of the house this morning between a double line of sufferers from mumps and influenza, and other pleasingly afflicted patients of yours, and I didn't like it very much."

"I don't believe they liked it much either," returned the Doctor. "One man with a sprained ankle told me about you. You shoved him in passing."

"Well, you can apologize to him in my behalf," returned the Idiot; "but you might add that he must expect very much the same treatment whenever he and a boy with mumps stand between me and the door. Sprained ankles aren't contagious, and I preferred shoving him to the other alternative."

The Doctor was silent, and the Idiot rose to go. "Where will the house be this evening about six-thirty, Mrs. Pedagog?" he asked, as he pushed his chair back from the table.

"Where? Why, here, of course," returned the landlady.

"Why, yes—of course," observed the Idiot, with an impatient gesture. "How foolish of me! I've really been so wrapped up in my canal-boat ideal that I came to believe that it might possibly be real and not a dream, after all. I almost believed that perhaps I should find that the house had been towed somewhere up into Westchester County on my return, so that we might all escape the city's tax on personal property, which I am told is unusually high this year."

With which sally the Idiot kissed his hand to Mr. Pedagog and retired from the scene.

II

"Let's write a book," suggested the Idiot, as he took his place at the board and unfolded his napkin.

"What about?" asked the Doctor, with a smile at the idea of the Idiot's thinking of embarking on literary pursuits.

"About four hundred pages long," said the Idiot. "I feel inspired."

"You are inspired," said the School-Master. "In your way you are a genius. I really never heard of such a variegated Idiot as you are in all my experience, and that means a great deal, I can tell you, for in the course of my career as an instructor of youth I have encountered many idiots."

"Were they idiots before or after having drank at the fount of your learning?" asked the Idiot, placidly.

Mr. Pedagog glared, and the Idiot was apparently satisfied. To make Mr. Pedagog glare appeared to be one of the chiefest of his ambitions.

"You will kindly remember, Mr. Idiot," said Mrs. Pedagog at this point, "that Mr. Pedagog is my husband, and such insinuations at my table are distinctly out of place."

"I ask your pardon, Mrs. Pedagog," rejoined the offender, meekly. "Nevertheless, as apart from the question in hand as to whether Mr. Pedagog inspires idiocy or not, I should like to get the views of this gathering on the point you make regarding the table. *Is* this your table? Is it not rather the table of those who sit about it to regale their inner man with the good things under which I remember once or twice in my life to have heard it groan? To my mind, the latter is the truth. It is *our* table, because we buy it, and I am forced to believe that some of us pay for it. I am prepared to admit that if Mr. Brief, for instance, is delinquent in his weekly payments, his interest in the table reverts to you until he shall have liquidated, and he is not privileged to say a word that you do not approve of; but I, for instance, who since January 1st have been compelled to pay in advance, am at least sole lessee, and for the time being proprietor of the portion for which I have paid. You have sold it to me. I have entered into possession, and while in possession, as a matter of right and not on sufferance, haven't I the privilege of freedom of speech?"

"You certainly exercise the privilege whether you have it or not," snapped Mr. Pedagog.

"Well, I believe in exercise," said the Idiot. "Exercise brings strength, and if exercising the privilege is going to strengthen it, exercise it I shall, if I have to hire a gymnasium for the purpose. But to return to Mrs. Pedagog's remark. It brings up another question that has more or less interested me. Because Mrs. Smithers married Mr. Pedagog, do we lose all of our rights in Mr. Pedagog? Before the happy event that reduced our number from ten to nine—"

"We are still ten, are we not?" asked Mr. Whitechoker, counting the guests.

"Not if Mr. Pedagog and the late Mrs. Smithers have become one," said the Idiot. "But, as I was saying, before the happy event that reduced our number from ten to nine we were permitted to address our friend Pedagog in any terms we saw fit, and whenever he became sufficiently interested to indulge in repartee we were privileged to return it. Have we relinquished that privilege? I don't remember to have done so."

"It's a question worthy of your giant intellect," said Mr. Pedagog, scornfully. "For myself, I do not at all object to anything you may choose to say to me or of me. Your assaults are to me as water is to a duck's back."

"I am sorry," said the Idiot. "I hate family disagreements, and here we have Mrs. Pedagog taking one side and Mr. Pedagog the other. But whatever decision may ultimately be reached, of one thing Mrs. Pedagog must be assured. I on principle side against Mr. Pedagog, and if it be the wish of my good landlady that I shall refrain from playing intellectual battledore and shuttlecock with her husband, whom we all revere, I certainly shall refrain. Hereafter if I indulge in anything that in any sense resembles repartee with our landlord, I wish it distinctly understood that an apology goes with it."

"That's all right, my boy," said the School-Master. "You mean well. You are a little new, that's all, and we all understand you."

"I don't understand him," growled the

Doctor, still smarting under the recollection of former breakfast-table discomfitures. "I wish we could get him translated."

"If you prescribed for me once or twice I think it likely I should be translated in short order," retorted the Idiot. "I wonder how I'd go translated into French?"

"You couldn't be expressed in French," put in the Lawyer. "It would take some barbarian tongue to do you justice."

"Very well," said the Idiot. "Proceed. Do me justice."

"I can't begin to," said Mr. Brief, angrily.

"That's what I thought," said the Idiot. "That's the reason why you always do me such great injustice. You lawyers always have to be doing something, even if it is only holding down a chair so that it won't blow out of your office window. If you haven't any justice to mete out, you take another tack and dispense injustice with lavish hand. However, I'll forgive you if you'll tell me one thing. What's libel, Mr. Brief?"

"None of your business," growled the Lawyer.

"A very good general definition," said the Idiot, approvingly. "If there's any business in the world that I should hate to have known as mine it is that of libel. I think, however, your definition is not definite. What I wanted to know was just how far I could go with remarks at this table and be safe from prosecution."

"Nobody would ever prosecute you, for two reasons," said the lawyer. "In a civil action for money damages a verdict against you for ten cents wouldn't be worth a rap, because the chances are you couldn't pay. In a criminal action your conviction would be a bad thing, because you would be likely to prove a corrupting influence in any jail in creation. Besides, you'd be safe before a jury, anyhow. You are just the sort of idiot that the intelligent jurors of to-day admire, and they'd acquit you of any crime. A man has a right to a trial at the hands of a jury of his peers. I don't think even in a jury-box twelve idiots equal to yourself could be found, so don't worry."

"Thanks. Have a cigarette?" said the Idiot, tossing one over to the Lawyer. "It's all I have. If I had a half-dollar I should pay you for your opinion; but since I haven't, I offer you my all. The temperature of my coffee seems to have fallen, Mrs. Pedagog. Will you kindly let me have another cup?"

"Certainly, said Mrs. Pedagog. "Mary, get the Idiot another cup."

Mary did as she was told, placing the empty bit of china at Mrs. Pedagog's side.

"It is for the Idiot, Mary," said Mrs. Pedagog, coldly. "Take it to him."

"Empty, ma'am?" asked the maid.

"Certainly, Mary," said the Idiot, perceiving Mrs. Pedagog's point. "I asked for another cup, not for more coffee."

Mrs. Pedagog smiled quietly at her own joke. At hair-splitting she could give the Idiot points.

"I am surprised that Mary should have thought I wanted more coffee," continued the Idiot, in an aggrieved tone. "It shows that she too thinks me out of my mind."

"You are not out of your mind," said the Bibliomaniac. "It would be a good thing if you were. In replenishing your mental supply you might have the luck to get better quality."

"I probably should have the luck," said the Idiot. "I have had a great store of it in my life. From the very start I have had luck. When I think that I was born myself, and not you, I feel as if I had had more than my share of good-fortune—more luck than the law allows. How much luck does the law allow, Mr. Brief?"

"Bosh!" said Mr. Brief, with a scornful wave of his hand, as if he were ridding himself of a troublesome gnat. "Don't bother me with such mind-withering questions."

"All right," said the Idiot. "I'll ask you an easier one. Why does not the world recognize matrimony?"

Mr. Whitechoker started. Here, indeed, was a novel proposition.

"I—I—must confess," said he, "that of all the idiotic questions I—er—I have ever had the honor of hearing asked that takes the—"

"Cake?" suggested the Idiot.

"—palm!" said Mr. Whitechoker, severely.

"Well, perhaps so," said the Idiot. "But matrimony is the science, or the art, or whatever you call it, of making two people one, is it not?"

"It certainly is," said Mr. Whitechoker. "But what of it?"

"The world does not recognize the unity," said the Idiot. "Take our good proprietors, for instance. They were made one by yourself, Mr. Whitechoker. I had the pleasure of being an usher at the ceremony, yielding the position of best man gracefully, as is my wont, to the Bibliomaniac. He was best man, but not the better man, by a simple process of reasoning. Now no one at this board disputes that Mr. and Mrs. Pedagog are one, but how about the world? Mr. Pedagog takes Mrs. Pedagog to a concert. Are they one there?"

"Why not?" asked Mr. Brief.

"That's what I want to know—why not? The world, as represented by the ticket-taker at the door, says they are not—or implies that they are not, by demanding tickets for two. They attempt to travel out to Niagara Falls. The railroad people charge them two fares; the hackman charges them two fares; the hotel bills are made out for two people. It is the same wherever they go in the world, and I regret to say that even in our own home there is a disposition to regard them as two. When I spoke of there being nine persons here instead of ten, Mr. Whitechoker himself disputed my point—and yet it was not so much his fault as the fault of Mr. and Mrs. Pedagog themselves. Mrs. Pedagog seems to cast doubt upon the unity by providing two separate chairs for the two halves that make up the charming entirety. Two cups are provided for their coffee. Two forks, two knives, two spoons, two portions of all the delicacies of the season which are lavished upon us out of season—generally after it—fall to their lot. They do not object to being called a happy *couple*, when they should be known as a happy single. Now what I want to know is why the world does not accept the shrinkage which has been pronounced valid by the church and is recognized by the individual? Can any one here tell me that?"

No one could, apparently. At least no one endeavored to. The Idiot looked inquiringly at all, and then, receiving no reply to his question, he rose from the table.

"I think," he said, as he started to leave the room—"I think we ought to write that book. If we made it up of the things you people don't know, it would be one of the greatest books of the century. At any rate, it would be great enough in bulk to fill the biggest library in America."

III

"I WISH I were beginning life all over again," said the Idiot one spring morning, as he took his accustomed place at Mrs. Pedagog's table.

"I wish you were," said Mr. Pedagog from behind his newspaper. "Then your parents would have you shut up in a nursery, and it is even conceivable that you would be receiving those disciplinary attentions with a slipper that you seem to me so frequently to deserve, were you at this present moment in the nursery stage of your development."

"My!" ejaculated the Idiot. "What a wonder you are, Mr. Pedagog! It is a good thing you are not a justice in a criminal court."

"And what, may I venture to ask," said Mr. Pedagog, glancing at the Idiot over his spectacles—"what has given rise to that extraordinary remark, the connection of which with anything that has been said or done this morning is distinctly not apparent?"

"I only meant that a man who was so given over to long sentences as you are would probably make too severe a judge in a criminal court," replied the Idiot, meekly. "Do you make use of the same phraseology in the class-room that you dazzle us with, I should like to know?"

"And why not, pray?" said Mr. Pedagog.

"No special reason," said the Idiot; "only it does seem to me that an instructor of youth ought to be more careful in his choice of adverbs than you appear to be. Of course Doctor Bolus here is under no obligation to speak more grammatically or correctly than he does. People call him in to prescribe, not to indulge in rhetorical periods, and he can write his prescriptions in a sort of intuitive Latin and nobody be the wiser, but you, who are said to be sowing the seeds of knowledge in the brain of youth, should be more careful."

"Hear the grammarian talk!" returned Mr. Pedagog. "Listen to this embryonic Samuel Johnson the Second. What have I said that so offends the linguistic taste of Lindley Murray, Jun.?"

"Nothing," returned the Idiot. "I cannot say that you have said anything. I never heard you say anything in my life ; but while you can no doubt find good authority for making use of the words 'distinctly not apparent,' you ought not to throw such phrases around carelessly. The thing which is distinct is apparent, therefore to say 'distinctly not apparent' to a mind that is not given to analysis sounds strange. You might as well say of a beautiful girl that she is plainly pretty, meaning of course that she is evidently pretty ; but those who are unacquainted with the idiomatic peculiarities of your speech might ask you if you meant that she was pretty in a plain sort of way. Suppose, too, you were writing a novel, and, in a desire to give your reader a fair idea of the personal appearance of a homely but good creature, you should say, 'It cannot be denied that Rosamond Follansbee was pretty plain ?' It wouldn't take a very grave error of the types to change your entire meaning. To save a line on a page, for instance, it might become necessary to eliminate a single word ; and if that word should chance to be the word 'plain' in the sentence I have given, your homely but good person would be set down as being undeniably pretty. Which shows, it seems to me, that too great care cannot be exercised in the making of selections from our vocabu—"

"You are the worst I *ever* knew!" snapped Mr. Pedagog.

"Which only proves," observed the Idiot, "that you have not heeded the Scriptural injunction that you should know thyself. Are those buckwheat cakes or doilies?"

Whether the question was heard or not is not known. It certainly was not answered, and silence reigned for a few minutes. Finally Mrs. Pedagog spoke, and in the manner of one who was somewhat embarrassed. "I am in an embarrassing position," said she.

"Good!" said the Idiot, *sotto-voce*, to the genial gentleman who occasionally imbibed. "There is hope for the landlady yet. If she can be embarrassed she is still human—a condition I was beginning to think she wotted not of."

"She whatted what?" queried the genial gentleman, not quite catching the Idiot's words.

"Never mind," returned the Idiot. "Let's hear how she ever came to be embarrassed."

"I have had an application for my first-floor suite, and I don't know whether I ought to accept it or not," said the landlady.

"She has a conscience, too," whispered the Idiot; and then he added, aloud, "And wherein lies the difficulty, Mrs. Pedagog?"

"The applicant is an actor; Junius Brutus Davenport is his name."

"A tragedian or a comedian?" asked the Bibliomaniac.

"Or first walking gentleman, who knows every railroad tie in the country?" put in the Idiot.

"That I do not know," returned the landlady. "His name sounds familiar enough, though. I thought perhaps some of you gentlemen might know of him."

"I have heard of Junius Brutus," observed the Doctor, chuckling slightly at his own humor, "and I've heard of Davenport, but Junius Brutus Davenport is a combination with which I am not familiar."

"Well, I can't see why it should make any difference whether the man is a tragedian, or a comedian, or a familiar figure to railroad men," said Mr. Whitechoker, firmly. "In any event, he would be an extremely objec—"

"It makes a great deal of difference," said the Idiot. "I've met tragedians, and I've met comedians, and I've met New York Central stars, and I can assure you they each represent a distinct type. The tragedians, as a rule, are quiet meek individuals, with soft low voices, in private life. They are more timid than otherwise, though essentially amiable. I knew a tragedian once who, after killing seventeen Indians, a road-agent, and a gross of cowboys between eight and ten P. M. every night for sixteen weeks, working six nights a week, was afraid of a mild little soft-shell crab that lay defenceless on a plate before him on the evening of the seventh night of the last week. Tragedians make agreeable companions, I can tell you ; and if J. Brutus Davenport is a tragedian, I think Mrs. Pedagog would do well to let him have the suite, provided, of course, that he pays for it in advance."

"I was about to observe, when our friend interrupted me," said Mr. Whitechoker, with dignity, "that in any event an actor at this board would be to me an extremely objec—"

"Now the comedians," resumed the Idiot, ignoring Mr. Whitechoker's remark—"the comedians are very different. They are twice as bloodthirsty as the murderers of the drama, and, worse than that, they are given to re-

"THEY ARE GIVEN TO REHEARSING AT ALL HOURS"

hearsing at all hours of the day and night. A tragedian is a hard character only on the stage, but the comedian is the comedian always. If we had one of those fellows in our midst, it would not be very long before we became part of the drama ourselves. Mrs. Pedagog would find herself embarrassed once an hour, instead of, as at present, once a century. Mr. Whitechoker would hear of himself as having appeared by proxy in a roaring farce before our comedian had been with us two months. The wise sayings of our friend the School-Master would be spoken nightly from the stage, to the immense delight of the gallery gods, and to the edification of the orchestra circle, who would wonder how so much information could have got into the world and they not know it before. The out-of-town papers would literally teem with witty extracts from our comedian's plays, which we should immediately recognize as the dicta of my poor self."

"All of which," put in Mr. Whitechoker, "but proves the truth of my assertion that such a person would be an extremely objec—"

"Then, as I said before," continued the Idiot, "he is continually rehearsing, and his objectionableness as a fellow-boarder would be greater or less, according to his play. If he were impersonating a shiftless wanderer, who shows remarkable bravery at a hotel fire, we should have to be prepared at any time to hear the fire-engines rushing up to the front door, and to see our comedian scaling the fire-escape with Mrs. Pedagog and her account-books in his arms, simply in the line of rehearsal. If he were impersonating a detective after a criminal masquerading as a good citizen, the School-Master would be startled some night by a hoarse voice at his key-hole exclaiming: 'Ha! ha! I have him now. There is no escape save by the back window, and that's so covered o'er with dust 'twere suffocation sure to try it.' I hesitate to say what would happen if he were a tank comedian."

"Perhaps," said Mr. Whitechoker, with a trifle more impatience than was compatible with his calling—" perhaps you will hesitate long enough for me to state what I have been trying to state ever since this soliloquy of yours began—that in any event, whether this person be a tragedian, or a comedian, or a walking gentleman, or a riding gentleman in a circus, I object to his being admitted to this circle, and I deem it well to say right here that as he comes in at the front door I go out at the back. As a clergyman, I do not approve of the stage."

"That ought to settle it," said the Idiot. "Mr. Whitechoker is too good a friend to us all here for us to compel him to go out of that back door into the rather limited market-garden Mrs. Pedagog keeps in the yard. My indirect plea for the admission of Mr. Junius Brutus Davenport was based entirely upon my desire to see this circle completed or nearer completion than it is at present. We have all the professions represented here but the stage, and why exclude it, granting that no one objects? The men whose lives are given over to the amusement of mankind, and who are willing to place themselves in the most outrageous situations night after night in order that we may for the time being seem to be lifted out of the unpleasant situations into which we have got ourselves, are in my opinion doing a noble work. The theatre enables us to woo forgetfulness of self successfully for a few brief hours, and I have seen the time when an hour or two of relief from actual cares has resulted in great good. Nevertheless, the gentleman is not elected; and if Mrs.

Pedagog will kindly refill my cup, I will ask you to join me in draining a toast to the health of the pastor of this flock, whose conscience, paradoxical as it may seem, is the most frequently worn and yet the least threadbare of the consciences represented at this table."

This easy settlement of her difficulty was so pleasing to Mrs. Pedagog that the Idiot's request was graciously acceded to, and Mr. Whitechoker's health was drank in coffee, after which the Idiot requested the genial gentleman who occasionally imbibed to join him privately in eating buckwheat cakes to the health of Mr. Davenport.

"I haven't any doubt that he is worthy of the attention," he said; "and if you will lend me the money to buy the tickets, I'll take you around to the Criterion to-night, where he is playing. I don't know whether he plays Hamlet or A Hole in the Roof; but, at any rate, we can have a good time between the acts."

IV

"I see the men are at work on the pavements this morning," said the School-Master, gazing out through the window at a number of laborers at work in the street.

"Yes," said the Idiot, calmly, "and I think Mrs. Pedagog ought to sue the Department of Public Works for libel. If she hasn't a case no maligned person ever had."

"What are you saying, sir?" queried the landlady, innocently.

"I say," returned the Idiot, pointing out into the street, "that you ought to sue the Department of Public Works for libel. They've got their sign right up against your house. *No Thorough Fare* is what it says. That's libel, isn't it, Mr. Brief?"

"It is certainly a fatal criticism of a boarding-house," observed Mr. Brief, with a twinkle in his eye, "but Mrs. Pedagog could hardly secure damages on that score."

"I don't know about that," returned the Idiot. "As I understand it, it is an old maxim of the law that the greater the truth the greater the libel. Mrs. Pedagog ought to receive a million— By-the-way, what have we this morning?"

"We have steak and fried potatoes, sir," replied Mrs. Pedagog, frigidly. "And I desire to add, that one who criticises the table as much as you do would do well to get his meals outside."

"That, Mrs. Pedagog, is not the point. The difficulty I find here lies in getting my meals inside," said the Idiot.

"Mary, you may bring in the mush," observed Mrs. Pedagog, pursing her lips, as she always did when she wished to show that she was offended.

"Yes, Mary," put in the School-Master; "let us have the mush as quickly as possible —and may it not be quite such mushy mush as the remarks we have just been favored with by our talented friend the Idiot."

"You overwhelm me with your compliments, Mr. Pedagog," replied the Idiot, cheerfully. "A flatterer like you should live in a flat."

"Has your friend completed his article on

old jokes yet?" queried the Bibliomaniac, with a smile and some apparent irrelevance.

"Yes and no," said the Idiot. "He has completed his labors on it by giving it up. He is a very thorough sort of a fellow, and he intended to make the article comprehensive, but he found he couldn't, because, judging from comments of men like you, for instance, he was forced to conclude that there never was a *new* joke. But, as I was saying the other morning—"

"Do you really remember what you say?" sneered Mr. Pedagog. "You must have a great memory for trifles."

"Sir, I shall never forget you," said the Idiot. "But to revert to what I was saying the other morning, I'd like to begin life all over again, so that I could prepare myself for the profession of architecture. It's the greatest profession in the world, and one which is surest to bring immortality to its successful follower. A man may write a splendid book, and become a great man for a while and within certain limits, but the chances are that some other man will come along later and supplant him. Then the book's sale will die out after a time, and with this will come a diminution of its author's reputation, in extent anyway. An actor or a great preacher becomes only a name after his death, but the architect who builds a cathedral or a fine public building really erects a monument to his own memory."

"He does if he can build it so that it will stay up," said the Bibliomaniac. "I think you, however, are better off as you are. If you had a more extended reputation or a lasting name you would probably be locked up in some retreat; or if you were not, posterity would want to know why."

"I am locked up in a retreat of Nature's making," said the Idiot, with a sigh. "Nature has set around me certain limitations which, while they are not material, might as well be so as far as my ability to soar above them is concerned—and it's well she has. If it were otherwise, my life would not be safe or bearable in this company. As it is, I am happy and not at all afraid of the effects your jealousy of me might entail if I were any better than the rest of you."

"I like that," said Mr. Pedagog.

"I thought you would," said the Idiot. "That's why I said it. I aim to please, and for once seem to have hit the bull's-eye. Mary, kindly break open this biscuit for me."

"Have you ideas on the subject of architecture that you so desire to become an architect?" queried Mr. Whitechoker, who was always full of sympathy for aspiring natures.

"A few," said the Idiot.

Mr. Pedagog laughed outright.

"Let's test his ideas," he said, in an amused way. "Take a cathedral, for instance. Suppose, Mr. Idiot, a man should come to you and say: 'Idiot, we have a fund of $800,000 in our hands, actual cash. We think of building a cathedral, and we think of employing you to draw up our plans. Give us some idea of what we should do.' Do you mean to tell me that you could say anything reasonable or intelligent to that man?"

"Well, that depends upon what you call reasonable and intelligent. I have never been able to find out what you mean by those terms," the Idiot answered, slowly. "But I could tell him something that I consider reasonable and intelligent."

"From your own point of view, then, as to reasonableness and intelligence, what should you say to him?"

"I'd make him out a plan providing for the investment of his $800,000 in five-percent. gold bonds, which would bring him in an income of $40,000 a year; after which I should call his attention to the fact that $40,000 a year would enable him to take 10,-000 poor children out of this sweltering city into the country, to romp and drink fresh milk and eat wholesome food for two weeks every summer from now until the end of time, which would build up a human structure that might be of more benefit to the world than any pile of bricks, marble, and wrought-iron I or any other architect could conceive of," said the Idiot. "The structure would stand up, too."

"You call that architecture, do you?" said Mr. Pedagog.

"Yes," said the Idiot, "of the renaissance order. But that, of course, you term idiocy — and maybe it is. I like to be that kind of an idiot. I do not claim to be able to build a cathedral, however. I don't suppose I could even build a boarding-house like this, but what I should like to do in architecture would be to put up a $5000 dwelling-house for $5000. That's a thing that has never been done, and I think I might be able to do it. If I did, I'd patent the plan and make a fortune. Then I should like to know enough about the science of planning a building to find out whether my model hotel is practicable or not."

"You have a model hotel in your mind, eh?" said the Bibliomaniac.

"It must be a very small hotel if it's in his mind," said the Doctor.

"That's tantamount to saying that it isn't anywhere," said Mr. Pedagog.

"Well, it's a great hotel just the same," said the Idiot. "Although I presume it would be expensive to build. It would have movable rooms, in the first place. Each room would be constructed like an elevator, with appliances at hand for moving it up and down. The great thing about this would be that persons could have a room on any floor they wanted it, so long as they got the room in the beginning. A second advantage would lie in the fact, that if you were sleeping in a room next door to another in which there was a crying baby, you could pull the rope and go up two or three flights until you were free from the noise. Then in case of fire the room in which the fire started could be lowered into a sliding tank large enough to immerse the whole thing in, which I should have constructed in the cellar. If the whole building were to catch fire, there would be no loss of life, because all the rooms could be lowered to the ground-floor, and the occupants could step right out upon solid ground. Then again, if you were down on the ground-floor, and desired to get an extended view of the surrounding country, it would be easy to raise your room to the desired elevation. Why, there's no end to the advantages to be gained from such an arrangement."

"It's a fine idea," said Mr. Pedagog, "and one worthy of your mammoth intellect. It couldn't possibly cost more than a million of dollars to erect such a hotel, could it?"

"No," said the Idiot. "And that is cheap alongside some of the hotels they are putting up nowadays."

"It could be built on less than four hundred acres of ground, too, I presume?" said the Bibliomaniac, with a wink at the Doctor.

"Certainly," said the Idiot, meekly.

"And if anybody fell sick in one of the rooms," said the Doctor, "and needed a change of air, you could have a tower over each, I suppose, so that the room could be elevated high enough to secure the different quality in the ether?"

"Undoubtedly," said the Idiot. "Although

that would add materially to the expense. A scarlet-fever patient, however, in a hotel like that could very easily be isolated from the rest of the house by the maintenance of what might be called the hospital floor."

"Superb!" said the Doctor. "I wonder you haven't spoken to some architectural friend about it."

"I have," said the Idiot. "You must remember that young fellow with a black mustache I had here to dinner last Saturday night."

"Yes, I remember him," said the Doctor. "Is he an architect?"

"He is—and a good one. He can take a brown-stone dwelling and turn it into a colonial mansion with a pot of yellow paint. He's a wonder. I submitted the idea to him."

"And what was his verdict?"

"I don't like to say," said the Idiot, blushing a little.

"Ha! ha!" laughed Mr. Pedagog. "I shouldn't think you would like to say. I guess we know what he said."

"I doubt it," said the Idiot; "but if you guess right, I'll tell you."

"He said you had better go and live in a

lunatic asylum," said Mr. Pedagog, with a chuckle.

"Not he," returned the Idiot, nibbling at his biscuit. "On the contrary. He advised me to stop living in one. He said contact with the rest of you was affecting my brain."

This time Mr. Pedagog did not laugh, but mistaking his coffee-cup for a piece of toast, bit a small section out of its rim ; and in the midst of Mrs. Pedagog's expostulation, which followed the School-Master's careless error, the Idiot and the Genial Old Gentleman departed, with smiles on their faces which were almost visible at the back of their respective necks.

V

"HULLO!" said the Idiot, as he began his breakfast. "This isn't Friday morning, is it? I thought it was Tuesday."

"So it is Tuesday," put in the School-Master.

"Then this fish is a little extra treat, is it?" observed the Idiot, turning with a smile to the landlady.

"Fish? That isn't fish, sir," returned the good lady. "That is liver."

"Oh, is it?" said the Idiot, apologetically. "Excuse me, my dear Mrs. Pedagog. I thought from its resistance that it was fried sole. Have you a hatchet handy?" he added, turning to the maid.

"My piece is tender enough. I can't see what you want," said the School-Master, coldly.

"I'd like your piece," replied the Idiot, suavely. "That is, if it really is tender enough."

"Don't pay any attention to him, my dear," said the School-Master to the landlady, whose ire was so very much aroused that she was about to make known her sentiments on certain subjects.

"No, Mrs. Pedagog," said the Idiot, "don't pay any attention to me, I beg of you. Anything that could add to the jealousy of Mr. Pedagog would redound to the discomfort of all of us. Besides, I really do not object to the liver. I need not eat it. And as for staying my appetite, I always stop on my way down-town after breakfast for a bite or two anyhow."

There was silence for a moment.

"I wonder why it is," began the Idiot, after tasting his coffee—"I wonder why it is Friday is fish-day all over the world, anyhow? Do you happen to be learned enough in piscatorial science to enlighten me on that point, Doctor?"

"No," returned the physician, gruffly. "I've never looked into the matter."

"I guess it's because Friday is an unlucky day," said the Idiot. "Just think of all the unlucky things that may happen before and after eating fish, as well as during the process. In the first place, before eating, you go off and fish all day, and have no luck—

don't catch a thing. You fall in the water perhaps, and lose your watch, or your fishhook catches in your coat-tails, with the result that you come near casting yourself instead of the fly into the brook or the pond, as the case may be. Perhaps the hook doesn't stop with the coat-tails, but goes on in, and catches you. That's awfully unlucky, especially when the hook is made of unusually barby barbed wire.

"Then, again, you may go fishing on somebody else's preserves, and get arrested, and sent to jail overnight, and hauled up the next morning, and have to pay ten dollars fine for poaching. Think of Mr. Pedagog being fined ten dollars for poaching! Awfully unfortunate!"

"Kindly leave me out of your calculations," returned Mr. Pedagog, with a flush of indignation.

"Certainly, if you wish it," said the Idiot. "We'll hand Mr. Brief over to the police, and let *him* be fined for poaching on somebody else's preserves—although that's sort of impossible, too, because Mrs. Pedagog never lets us see preserves of any kind."

"We had brandied peaches last Sunday night," said the landlady, indignantly.

"Oh yes, so we did," returned the Idiot. "That must have been what the Bibliomaniac had taken," he added, turning to the genial gentleman who occasionally imbibed. "You know, we thought he'd been—ah—he'd been absorbing."

"To what do you refer?" asked the Bibliomaniac, curtly.

"To the brandied peaches," returned the Idiot. "Do not press me further, please, because we like you, old fellow, and I don't believe anybody noticed it but ourselves."

"Noticed what? I want to know what you noticed and when you noticed it," said the Bibliomaniac, savagely. "I don't want any nonsense, either. I just want a plain statement of facts. What did you notice?"

"Well, if you must have it," said the Idiot, slowly, "my friend who imbibes and I were rather pained on Sunday night to observe that you—that you had evidently taken something rather stronger than cold water, tea, or Mr. Pedagog's opinions."

"It's a libel, sir!—a gross libel!" retorted the Bibliomaniac. "How did I show it? That's what I want to know. How—did—I —show—it? Speak up quick, and loud too. How did I show it?"

HE COULD BE HEARD THROWING THINGS ABOUT

"Well, you went up-stairs after tea."

"Yes, sir, I did."

"And my friend who imbibes and I were left down in the front hall, and while we were talking there you put your head over the banisters and asked, 'Who's that down there?' Remember that?"

"Yes, sir, I do. And you replied, 'Mr. Auburnose and myself.'"

"Yes. And then you asked, 'Who are the other two?'"

"Well, I did. What of it?"

"Mr. Auburnose and I were there alone. That's what of it. Now I put a charitable construction on the matter and say it was the peaches, when you fly off the handle like one of Mrs. Pedagog's coffee-cups."

"Sir!" roared the Bibliomaniac, jumping from his chair. "You are the greatest idiot I know."

"Sir!" returned the Idiot, "you flatter me."

But the Bibliomaniac was not there to hear. He had rushed from the room, and during the deep silence that ensued he could be heard throwing things about in the chamber overhead, and in a very few moments the banging of the front door and scurrying down the brown stone steps showed that he had gone out of doors to cool off.

"It is too bad," said the Idiot, after a while, "that he has such a quick temper. It doesn't do a bit of good to get mad that way. He'll be uncomfortable all day long, and over what? Just because I attempted to say a good word for him, and announce the restoration of my confidence in his temperance qualities, he cuts up a high-jinks that makes everybody uncomfortable.

"But to resume about this fish business," continued the Idiot. "Fish—"

"Oh, fish be hanged!" said the Doctor, impatiently. "We've had enough of fish."

"Very well," returned the idiot; "as you wish. Hanging isn't the best treatment for fish, but we'll let that go. I never cared for the finny tribe myself, and if Mrs. Pedagog can be induced to do it, I for one am in favor of keeping shad, shark, and shrimps out of the house altogether."

VI

THE Idiot was unusually thoughtful—a fact which made the School-Master and the Bibliomaniac unusually nervous. Their stock criticism of him was that he was thoughtless; and yet when he so far forgot his natural propensities as to meditate, they did not like it. It made them uneasy. They had a haunting fear that he was conspiring with himself against them, and no man, not even a callous school-master or a confirmed bibliomaniac, enjoys feeling that he is the object of a conspiracy. The thing to do, then, upon this occasion, seemed obviously to interrupt his train of thought—to put obstructions upon his mental track, as it were, and ditch the express, which they feared was getting up steam at that moment to run them down.

"You don't seem quite yourself this morning, sir," said the Bibliomaniac.

"Don't I?" queried the Idiot. "And whom do I seem to be?"

"I mean that you seem to have something on your mind that worries you," said the Bibliomaniac.

"No, I haven't anything on my mind," returned the Idiot. "I was thinking about you and Mr. Pedagog—which implies a thought not likely to use up much of my gray matter."

"Do you think your head holds any gray matter?" put in the Doctor.

"Rather verdant, I should say," said Mr. Pedagog.

"Green, gray, or pink," said the Idiot, "choose your color. It does not affect the fact that I was thinking about the Bibliomaniac and Mr. Pedagog. I have a great scheme in hand, which only requires capital and the assistance of those two gentlemen to launch it on the sea of prosperity. If any of you gentlemen want to get rich and die in comfort as the owner of your homes, now is your chance."

"In what particular line of business is your scheme?" asked Mr. Whitechoker. He had often felt that he would like to die in comfort, and to own a little house, even if it had a large mortgage on it.

"Journalism," said the Idiot. "There is a pile of money to be made out of journalism, particularly if you happen to strike a new idea. Ideas count."

"How far up do your ideas count—up to five?" questioned Mr. Pedagog, with a tinge of sarcasm in his tone.

"I don't know about that," returned the Idiot. "The idea I have hold of now, however, will count up into the millions if it can only be set going, and before each one of those millions will stand a big capital S with two black lines drawn vertically through it—in other words, my idea holds dollars, but to get the crop you've got to sow the seed. Plant a thousand dollars in my idea, and next year you'll reap two thousand. Plant that, and next year you'll have four thousand, and so on. At that rate millions come easy."

"I'll give you a dollar for the idea," said the Bibliomaniac.

"No, I don't want to sell. You'll do to help develop the scheme. You'll make a first-rate tool, but you aren't the workman to manage the tool. I will go as far as to say, however, that without you and Mr. Pedagog, or your equivalents in the animal kingdom, the idea isn't worth the fabulous sum you offer."

"You have quite aroused my interest," said Mr. Whitechoker. "Do you propose to start a new paper?"

"You are a good guesser," replied the Idiot. "That is a part of the scheme—but it isn't the idea. I propose to start a new paper in accordance with the plan which the idea contains."

"Is it to be a magazine, or a comic paper, or what?" asked the Bibliomaniac.

"Neither. It's a daily."

"That's nonsense," said Mr. Pedagog, putting his spoon into the condensed-milk can by mistake. "There isn't a single scheme in daily journalism that hasn't been tried—except printing an evening paper in the morning."

"That's been tried," said the Idiot. "I know of an evening paper the second edition of which is published at mid-day. That's an old dodge, and there's money in it, too—money that will never be got out of it. But I really have a grand scheme. So many of our dailies, you know, go in for every horrid detail of daily events that people are beginning to tire of them. They contain practically the same things day after day. So many columns of murder, so many beautiful suicides, so much sport, a modicum of general intelligence, plenty of fires, no end of embezzlements, financial news, advertisements, and head-lines. Events, like history, repeat themselves, until people have grown weary of them. They want something new. For instance, if you read in your morning paper that a man has shot another man, you know that the man who was shot was an inoffensive person who never injured a soul, stood high in the community in which he lived, and leaves a widow with four children. On the other hand, you know without reading the account that the murderer shot his victim in self-defence, and was apprehended by the detectives late last night; that his counsel forbid him to talk to the reporters, and that it is rumored that he comes of a good family living in New England.

"If a breach of trust is committed, you know that the defaulter was the last man of whom such an act would be suspected, and, except in the one detail of its location and sect, that he was prominent in some church. You can calculate to a cent how much has been stolen by a glance at the amount of space devoted to the account of the crime. Loaf of bread, two lines. Thousand dollars, ten lines. Hundred thousand dollars, half-column. Million dollars, a full column. Five million dollars, half the front page, wood-cut of the embezzler, and two editorials, one leader and one paragraph.

"And so with everything. We are creatures of habit. The expected always happens, and newspapers are dull because the events they chronicle are dull."

"Granting the truth of this," put in the School-Master, "what do you propose to do?"

"Get up a newspaper that will devote its space to telling what hasn't happened."

"That's been done," said the Bibliomaniac.

"To a much more limited extent than we think," returned the Idiot. "It has never been done consistently and truthfully."

"I fail to see how a newspaper can be made to prevaricate truthfully," asserted Mr. Whitechoker. To tell the truth, he was greatly disappointed with the idea, because he could not in the nature of things become one of its beneficiaries.

"I haven't suggested prevarication," said the Idiot. "Put on your front page, for instance, an item like this: 'George Bronson, colored, aged twenty-nine, a resident of Thompson Street, was caught cheating at poker last night. He was not murdered.' There you tell what has not happened. There is a variety about it. It has the charm of the unexpected. Then you might say: 'Curious incident on Wall Street yesterday. So-and-so, who was caught on the bear side of the market with 10,000 shares of J. B. & S. K. W., paid off all his obligations in full, and retired from business with $1,000,000 clear.' Or we might say, 'Superintendent Smithers, of the St. Goliath's Sunday-school, who is also cashier in the Forty-eighth National Bank, has not absconded with $4,000,000.'"

"Oh, that's a rich idea," put in the School-Master. "You'd earn $1,000,000 in libel suits the first year."

"No, you wouldn't, either," said the Idiot. "You don't libel a man when you say he hasn't murdered anybody. Quite the contrary, you call attention to his conspicuous virtue. You are in reality commending those who refrain from criminal practice, instead of delighting those who are fond of departing from the paths of Christianity by giving them notoriety."

"But I fail to see in what respect Mr. Pedagog and I are essential to your scheme," said the Bibliomaniac.

"I must confess to some curiosity on my own part on that point," added the School-Master.

"Why, it's perfectly clear," returned the Idiot, with a conciliating smile as he prepared to depart. "You both know so much that isn't so, that I rather rely on you to fill up."

VII

A NEW boarder had joined the circle about Mrs. Pedagog's breakfast-table. He had what the Idiot called a three-ply name—which was Richard Henderson Warren—and he was by profession a poet. Whether it was this that made it necessary for him to board or not, the rewards of the muse being rather slender, was known only to himself, and he showed no disposition to enlighten his fellow-boarders on the subject. His success as a poet Mrs. Pedagog found it hard to gauge; for while the postman left almost daily numerous letters, the envelopes of which showed that they came from the various periodicals of the day, it was never exactly clear whether or not the missives contained remittances or rejected manuscripts, though the fact that Mr. Warren was the only boarder in the house who had requested to have a waste-basket added to the furniture of his room seemed to indicate that they contained the latter. To this request Mrs. Pedagog had gladly acceded, because she had a notion that therein at some time or another would be found a clew to the new boarder's past history—or possibly some evidence of such duplicity as the good lady suspected he might be guilty of. She had read that Byron was profligate, and that Poe was addicted to drink, and she was impressed with the idea that poets generally were bad men, and she regarded the waste-basket as a possible means of protecting herself against any such idiosyncrasies of her new-found genius as would operate to her disadvantage if not looked after in time.

This waste-basket she made it her daily duty to empty, and in the privacy of her own room. Half-finished "ballads, songs, and snatches" she perused before consigning them to the flames or to the large jute bag in the cellar, for which the ragman called two or three times a year. Once Mrs. Pedagog's heart almost stopped beating when she found at the bottom of the basket a printed slip beginning, "*The Editor regrets that the enclosed lines are unavailable,*" and closing with about thirteen reasons, any one or all of which might have been the main cause of the poet's disappointment. Had it not been for the kindly clause in the printed slip that insinuated in graceful terms that this rejection did not imply a lack of literary merit in the contribution itself, the good lady, knowing well that there was even less money to be made from rejected than from accepted poetry, would have been inclined to request the poet to vacate the premises. The very next day, however, she was glad she had not requested the resignation of the poet from the laureateship of her house; for the same basket gave forth another printed slip from another editor, begging the poet to accept the enclosed check, with thanks for his contribution, and asking him to deposit it as soon as practicable — which was pleasing enough, since it implied that the poet was the possessor of a bank account.

Now Mrs. Pedagog was consumed with curiosity to know for how large a sum the check called—which desire was gratified a few days later, when the inspired boarder paid his week's bill with three one-dollar bills and a check, signed by a well-known publisher, for two dollars.

By the boarders themselves the poet was regarded with much interest. The School-Master had read one or two of his effusions in the Fireside Corner of the journal he received weekly from his home up in New England—effusions which showed no little merit, as well as indicating that Mr. Warren wrote for a literary syndicate; Mr. Whitechoker had known of him as the young man who was to have written a Christmas carol for his Sunday-school a year before, and who had finished and presented the manuscript shortly after New-Year's day; while to the Idiot, Mr. Warren's name was familiar as that of a frequent contributor to the funny papers of the day.

"I was very much amused by your poem in the last number of the *Observer*, Mr. Warren," said the Idiot, as they sat down to breakfast together.

"Were you, indeed?" returned Mr. Warren. "I am sorry to hear that, for it was intended to be a serious effort."

"Of course it was, Mr. Warren, and so it appeared," said the School-Master, with an indignant glance at the Idiot. "It was a very dignified and stately bit of work, and I must congratulate you upon it."

"I didn't mean to give offence," said the Idiot. "I've read so much of yours that was purely humorous that I believe I'd laugh at a dirge if you should write one; but I really thought your lines in the *Observer* were a burlesque. You had the same thought that Rossetti expresses in 'The Woodspurge':

> 'The wind flapped loose, the wind was still,
> Shaken out dead from tree to hill;
> I had walked on at the wind's will,
> I sat now, for the wind was still.'

That's Rossetti, if you remember. Slightly suggestive of 'Blow Ye Winds of the Morning! Blow! Blow! Blow!' but more or less pleasing."

"I recall the poem you speak of," said Warren, with dignity; "but the true poet, sir—and I hope I have some claim to be considered as such—never so far forgets himself as to burlesque his masters."

"Well, I don't know what to call it, then, when a poet takes the same thought that has previously been used by his masters and makes a funny poem—"

"But," returned the Poet, warmly, "it was not a funny poem."

"It made me laugh," retorted the Idiot,

"and that is more than half the professedly funny poems we get nowadays can do. Therefore I say it was a funny poem, and I don't see how you can deny that it was a burlesque of Rossetti."

"Well, I do deny it *in toto*."

"I don't know anything about denying it *in toto*," rejoined the Idiot, "but I'd deny it in print if I were you. I know plenty of people who think it was a burlesque, and I overheard one man say — he is a Rossetti crank — that you ought to be ashamed of yourself for writing it."

"There is no use of discussing the matter further," said the Poet. "I am innocent of any such intent as you have ascribed to me, and if people say I have burlesqued Rossetti they say what is not true."

"Did you ever read that little poem of Swinburne's called 'The Boy at the Gate'?" asked the Idiot, to change the subject.

"I have no recollection of it," said the Poet, shortly.

"The name sounds familiar," put in Mr. Whitechoker, anxious not to be left out of a literary discussion.

"I have read it, but I forget just how it goes," vouchsafed the School-Master, forgetting for a moment the Robert Elsmere episode and its lesson.

"It goes something like this," said the Idiot:

"Sombre and sere the slim sycamore sighs;
Lushly the lithe leaves lie low o'er the land;
Whistles the wind with its whisperings wise,
Grewsomely gloomy and garishly grand.
So doth the sycamore solemnly stand,
Wearily watching in wondering wait;
So it has stood for six centuries, and
Still it is waiting the boy at the gate."

"No; I never read the poem," said Mr. Whitechoker, "but I'd know it was Swinburne in a minute. He has such a command of alliterative language."

"Yes," said the Poet, with an uneasy glance at the Idiot. "It is Swinburnian; but what was the poem about?"

"'The boy at the gate,'" said the Idiot. "The idea was that the sycamore was standing there for centuries waiting for the boy who never turns up."

"It really is a beautiful thought," put in Mr. Whitechoker. "It is, I presume, an allegory to contrast faithful devotion and constancy with unfaithfulness and fickleness.

Such thoughts occur only to the wholly gifted. It is only to the poetic temperament that the conception of such a thought can come coupled with the ability to voice it in fitting terms. There is a grandeur about the lines the Idiot has quoted that betrays the master-mind."

"Very true," said the School-Master, "and I take this opportunity to say that I am most agreeably surprised in the Idiot. It is no small thing even to be able to repeat a poet's lines so carefully, and with so great lucidity, and so accurately, as I can testify that he has just done."

"Don't be too pleased, Mr. Pedagog," said the Idiot, dryly. "I only wanted to show Mr. Warren that you and Mr. Whitechoker, mines of information though you are, have not as yet worked up a corner on knowledge to the exclusion of the rest of us." And with these words the Idiot left the table.

"He is a queer fellow," said the School-Master. "He is full of pretence and hollowness, but he is sometimes almost brilliant."

"What you say is very true," said Mr. Whitechoker. "I think he has just escaped being a smart man. I wish we could take him in hand, Mr. Pedagog, and make him more of a fellow than he is."

Later in the day the Poet met the Idiot on the stairs. "I say," he said, "I've looked all through Swinburne, and I can't find that poem."

"I know you can't," returned the Idiot, "because it isn't there. Swinburne never wrote it. It was a little thing of my own. I was only trying to get a rise out of Mr. Pedagog and his Reverence with it. You have frequently appeared impressed by the undoubtedly impressive manner of these two gentlemen. I wanted to show you what their opinions were worth."

"Thank you," returned the Poet, with a smile. "Don't you want to go into partnership with me and write for the funny papers? It would be a splendid thing for me—your ideas are so original."

"And I can see fun in everything, too," said the Idiot, thoughtfully.

"Yes," returned the Poet. "Even in my serious poems."

Which remark made the Idiot blush a little, but he soon recovered his composure and made a firm friend of the Poet.

The first fruits of the partnership have not yet appeared, however.

As for Messrs. Whitechoker and Pedagog, when they learned how they had been deceived, they were so indignant that they did not speak to the Idiot for a week.

VIII

It was Sunday morning, and Mr. Whitechoker, as was his wont on the first day of the week, appeared at the breakfast table severe as to his mien.

"Working on Sunday weighs on his mind," the Idiot said to the Bibliomaniac, "but I don't see why it should. The luxury of rest that he allows himself the other six days of the week is surely an atonement for the hours of labor he puts in on Sunday."

But it was not this that on Sunday mornings weighed on the mind of the Reverend Mr. Whitechoker. He appeared more serious of visage then because he had begun to think of late that his fellow-boarders lived too much in the present, and ignored almost totally that which might be expected to come. He had been revolving in his mind for several weeks the question as to whether it was or was not his Christian duty to attempt to influence the lives of these men with whom the chances of life had brought him in contact. He had finally settled it to his own satisfaction that it was his duty so to do, and he had resolved, as far as lay in his power, to direct the conversation at Sunday morning's breakfast into spiritual rather than into temporal matters.

So, as Mrs. Pedagog was pouring the coffee, Mr. Whitechoker began:

"Do you gentlemen ever pause in your every-day labors and thought to let your minds rest upon the future — the possibilities it has in store for us, the consequences which—"

"No mush, thank you," said the Idiot. Then turning to Mr. Whitechoker, he added: "I can't answer for the other gentlemen at this board, but I can assure you, Mr. Whitechoker, that I often do so. It was only last night, sir, that my genial friend who imbibes and I were discussing the future and its possibilities, and I venture to assert that there is no more profitable food for reflection anywhere in the larders of the mind than that."

"Larders of the mind is excellent," said the School-Master, with a touch of sarcasm in his voice. "Perhaps you would not mind opening the door to your mental pantry, and letting us peep within at the stores you keep there. I am sure that on the subject in hand your views cannot fail to be original as well as edifying."

"I am also sure," said Mr. Whitechoker, somewhat surprised to hear the Idiot speak as he did, having sometimes ventured to doubt if that flippant-minded young man ever reflected on the serious side of life—"I am also sure that it is most gratifying to hear that you have done some thinking on the subject."

"I am glad you are gratified, Mr. Whitechoker," replied the Idiot, "but I am far from taking undue credit to myself because I reflect upon the future and its possibilities. I do not see how any man can fail to be interested in the subject, particularly when he considers the great strides science has made in the last twenty years."

"I fail to see," said the School-Master, "what the strides of science have to do with it."

"You fail to see so often, Mr. Pedagog," returned the Idiot, "that I would advise your eyes to make an assignment in favor of your pupils."

"I must confess," put in Mr. Whitechoker, blandly, "that I too am somewhat—er—somewhat—"

"Somewhat up a tree as to science's connection with the future?" queried the Idiot.

"You have my meaning, but hardly the phraseology I should have chosen," replied the minister.

"My style is rather epigrammatic," said the Idiot, suavely. "I appreciate the flattery implied by your noticing it. But science has everything to do with it. It is science that is going to make the future great. It is science that has annihilated distance, and the annihilation has just begun. Twenty years ago it was hardly possible for a man standing on one side of the street to make himself heard on the other, the acoustic properties of the atmosphere not being what they should be. To-day you can stand in the pulpit of your church, and by means of certain scientific apparatus make yourself heard in Boston, New Orleans, or San Francisco. Has this no bearing on the future? The time will come, Mr. Whitechoker, when your missionaries will be able to sit in their comfortable rectories, and ring up the heathen in foreign climes, and convert them over the telephone, without running the slightest danger of falling into the soup, which expression I use in its literal rather than in its metaphorical sense."

"But—" interrupted Mr. Whitechoker.

"Now wait, please," said the Idiot. "If science can annihilate degrees of distance, who shall say that before many days science may not annihilate degrees of time? If San Francisco, thousands of miles distant, can be brought within range of the ear, why cannot 1990 be brought before the mind's eye? And if 1990 can be brought before the mind's eye, what is to prevent the invention of a prophetograph which shall enable us to cast a horoscope which shall reach all around eternity and half-way back, if not further?"

"You do not understand me," said Mr. Whitechoker. "When I speak of the future, I do not mean the temporal future."

"I know exactly what you mean," said the Idiot. "I've dealt in futures, and I am familiar with all kinds. It is you, sir, that do not understand me. My claim is perfectly plausible, and in its results is bound to make the world better. Do you suppose that any man who, by the aid of my prophetograph, sees that on a certain date in the future he will be hanged for murder is going to fail to provide himself with an alibi in regard to that particular murder, and must we not admit that having provided himself with that alibi he will of necessity avoid bloodshed, and so avoid the gallows? That's reasonable. So in regard to all the thousand and one other peccadilloes that go to make this life a sinful one. Science, by a purely logical advance along the lines already mapped out for itself, and in part already traversed, will enable men to avoid the pitfalls and reap only the windfalls of life; we shall all see what terrible consequences await on a single misstep, and we shall not make the misstep. Can you still claim that science and the future have nothing to do with each other?"

"You are talking of matters purely temporal," said Mr. Whitechoker. "I have reference to our spiritual future."

"And the two," observed the Idiot, "are so closely allied that we cannot separate them. The proverb about looking after the pennies and letting the pounds take care of themselves applies here. I believe that if I take care of my temporal future — which, by-the-way, does not exist—my spiritual future will take care of itself; and if science places the hereafter before us—and you admit that even now it is before us — all we have to do is to take advantage of our opportunities, and mend our lives accordingly."

"But if science shows you what is to come," said the School-Master, "it must show your fate with perfect accuracy, or it ceases to be science, in which event your entertaining notions as to reform and so on are entirely fallacious."

"Not at all," said the Idiot. "We are approaching the time when science, which is much more liberal than any other branch of knowledge, will sacrifice even truth itself for the good of mankind."

"You ought to start a paradox company," suggested the Doctor.

"Either that or make himself the nucleus of an insane asylum," observed the School-Master, viciously. "I never knew a man with such maniacal views as those we have heard this morning."

"There is a great deal, Mr. Pedagog, that you have never known," returned the Idiot. "Stick by me, and you'll die with a mind richly stored."

Whereat the School-Master left the table with such manifest impatience that Mr. Whitechoker was sorry he had started the conversation.

The genial gentleman who occasionally imbibed and the Idiot withdrew to the latter's room, where the former observed:

"What are you driving at, anyhow? Where did you get those crazy ideas?"

"I ate a Welsh-rarebit last night, and dreamed 'em," returned the Idiot.

"I thought as much," said his companion. "What deuced fine things dreams are, anyhow!"

IX

Breakfast was very nearly over, and it was of such exceptionally good quality that very few remarks had been made. Finally the ball was set rolling by the Lawyer.

"How many packs of cigarettes do you smoke a day?" he asked, as the Idiot took one from his pocket and placed it at the side of his coffee-cup.

"Never more than forty-six," said the Idiot. "Why? Do you think of starting a cigarette stand?"

"Not at all," said Mr. Brief. "I was only wondering what chance you had to live to maturity, that's all. Your maturity period will be in about eight hundred and sixty years from now, the way I calculate, and it seemed to me that, judging from the number of cigarettes you smoke, you were not likely to last through more than two or three of those years."

"Oh, I expect to live longer than that," said the Idiot. "I think I'm good for at least four years. Don't you, Doctor?"

"I decline to have anything to say about your case," retorted the Doctor, whose feeling towards the Idiot was not surpassingly affectionate.

"In that event I shall probably live five years more," said the Idiot.

The Doctor's lip curled, but he remained silent.

"You'll live," put in Mr. Pedagog, with a chuckle. "The good die young."

"How did you happen to keep alive all this time then, Mr. Pedagog?" asked the Idiot.

"I have always eschewed tobacco in every form, for one thing," said Mr. Pedagog.

"I am surprised," put in the Idiot. "That's really a bad habit, and I marvel greatly that you should have done it."

The School-Master frowned, and looked at the Idiot over the rims of his glasses, as was his wont when he was intent upon getting explanations.

"Done what?" he asked, severely.

"Chewed tobacco," replied the Idiot. "You just said that one of the things that has kept you lingering in this vale of tears was that you have always chewed tobacco. I never did that, and I never shall do it, because I deem it a detestable diversion."

"I didn't say anything of the sort," retorted Mr. Pedagog, getting red in the face. "I never said that I chewed tobacco in any form."

"Oh, come!" said the Idiot, with well-feigned impatience, "what's the use of talking that way? We all heard what you said, and I have no doubt that it came as a shock to every member of this assemblage. It certainly was a shock to me, because, with all my weaknesses and bad habits, I think tobacco-chewing unutterably bad. The worst part of it is that you chew it in every form. A man who chews chewing-tobacco only may some time throw off the habit, but when one gets to be such a victim to it that he chews up cigars and cigarettes and plugs of pipe tobacco, it seems to me he is incurable. It is not only a bad habit then; it amounts to a vice."

Mr. Pedagog was getting apoplectic. "You know well enough that I never said the words you attribute to me," he said, sternly.

"Really, Mr. Pedagog," returned the Idiot,

with an irritating shake of his head, as if he were confidentially hinting to the School-Master to keep quiet—"really you pain me by these futile denials. Nobody forced you into the confession. You made it entirely of your own volition. Now I ask you, as a man and brother, what's the use of saying anything more about it? We believe you to be a person of the strictest veracity, but when you say a thing before a tableful of listeners one minute, and deny it the next, we are forced to one of two conclusions, neither of which is pleasing. We must conclude that either, repenting your confession, you sacrifice the truth, or that the habit to which you have confessed has entirely destroyed your perception of the moral question involved. Undue use of tobacco has, I believe, driven men crazy. Opium-eating has destroyed all regard for truth in one whose word had always been regarded as good as a government bond. I presume the undue use of tobacco can accomplish the same sad result. By-the-way, did you ever try opium?"

"Opium is ruin," said the Doctor, Mr. Pedagog's indignation being so great that he seemed to be unable to find the words he was evidently desirous of hurling at the Idiot.

"It is, indeed," said the Idiot. "I knew a man once who smoked one little pipeful of it, and, while under its influence, sat down at his table and wrote a story of the supernatural order that was so good that everybody said he must have stolen it from Poe or some other master of the weird, and now nobody will have anything to do with him. Tobacco, however, in the sane use of it, is a good thing. I don't know of anything that is more satisfying to the tired man than to lie back on a sofa, of an evening, and puff clouds of smoke and rings into the air. One of the finest dreams I ever had came from smoking. I had blown a great mountain of smoke out into the room, and it seemed to become real, and I climbed to its summit and saw the most beautiful country at my feet— a country in which all men were happy, where there were no troubles of any kind, where no whim was left ungratified, where jealousies were not, and where every man who made more than enough to live on paid the surplus into the common treasury for the use of those who hadn't made quite enough. It was a national realization of the golden rule, and I maintain that if smoking were bad nothing so good, even in the abstract form of an idea, could come out of it."

"That's a very nice thought," said the Poet. "I'd like to put that into verse. The idea of a people dividing up their surplus of wealth among the less successful strugglers is beautiful."

"You can have it," said the Idiot, with a pleased smile. "I don't write poetry of that kind myself unless I work hard, and I've found that when the poet works hard he produces poems that read hard. You are welcome to it. Another time I was dreaming over my cigar, after a day of the hardest kind of trouble at the office. Everything had gone wrong with me, and I was blue as indigo. I came home here, lit a cigar, and threw myself down upon my bed and began to puff. I felt like a man in a deep pit, out of which there was no way of getting. I closed my eyes for a second, and to all intents and purposes I lay in that pit. And then what did tobacco do for me? Why, it lifted me right out of my prison. I thought I was sitting on a rock down in the depths. The stars twinkled tantalizingly above me. They invited me to freedom, knowing that freedom was not attainable. Then I blew a ring of smoke from my mouth, and it began to rise slowly at first, and then, catching in a current of air, it flew upward more rapidly, widening constantly, until it disappeared in the darkness above. Then I had a thought. I filled my mouth as full of smoke as possible, and blew forth the greatest ring you ever saw, and as it started to rise I grasped it in my two hands. It struggled beneath my weight, lengthened out into an elliptical link, and broke, and let me down with a dull thud. Then I made two rings, grasping one with my left hand and the other with my right—"

"And they lifted you out of the pit, I suppose?" sneered the Bibliomaniac.

"I do not say that they did," said the Idiot, calmly. "But I do know that when I opened my eyes I wasn't in the pit any longer, but up-stairs in my hall-bedroom."

"How awfully mysterious!" said the Doctor, satirically.

"Well, I don't approve of smoking," said Mr. Whitechoker. "I agree with the London divine who says it is the pastime of perdition. It is not prompted by natural instincts. It is only the habit of artificial civilization. Dogs and horses and birds get along without it. Why shouldn't man?"

"Hear! hear!" cried Mr. Pedagog, clapping his hands approvingly.

"Where? where?" put in the Idiot. "That's a great argument. Dog's don't put up in boarding-houses. Is the boarding-house, therefore, the result of a degraded, artificial civilization? I have seen educated horses that didn't smoke, but I have never seen an educated horse, or an uneducated one, for that matter, that had even had the chance to smoke, or the kind of mouth that would enable him to do it in case he had the chance. I have also observed that horses don't read books, that birds don't eat mutton-chops, that dogs don't go to the opera, that donkeys don't play the piano—at least, four-legged donkeys don't—so you might as well argue that since horses, dogs, birds, and donkeys get along without literature, music, mutton-chops, and piano-playing—"

"You've covered music," put in the Lawyer, who liked to be precise.

"True; but piano-playing isn't always music," returned the Idiot. "You might as well argue because the beasts and the birds do without these things man ought to. Fish don't smoke, neither do they join the police-force, therefore man should neither smoke nor become a guardian of the peace."

"Nevertheless it is a pastime of perdition," insisted Mr. Whitechoker.

"No, it isn't," retorted the Idiot. "Smoking is the business of perdition. It smokes because it has to."

"There! there!" remonstrated Mr. Pedagog.

"You mean hear! hear! I presume," said the Idiot.

"I mean that you have said enough!" remarked Mr. Pedagog, sharply.

"Very well," said the Idiot. "If I have convinced you all I am satisfied, not to say gratified. But really, Mr. Pedagog," he added, rising to leave the room, "if I were you I'd give up the practice of chewing—"

"Hold on a minute, Mr. Idiot," said Mr. Whitechoker, interrupting. He was desirous that Mr. Pedagog should not be further irritated. "Let me ask you one question. Does your old father smoke?"

"No," said the Idiot, leaning easily over the back of his chair—"no. What of it?"

"Nothing at all—except that perhaps if he could get along without it you might," suggested the clergyman.

"He couldn't get along without it if he knew what good tobacco was," said the Idiot.

"Then why don't you introduce him to it?" asked the Minister.

"Because I do not wish to make him unhappy," returned the Idiot, softly. "He thinks his seventy years have been the happiest years that any mortal ever had, and if now in his seventy-first year he discovered that during the whole period of his manhood he had been deprived through ignorance of so great a blessing as a good cigar, he'd become like the rest of us, living in anticipation of delights to come, and not finding approximate bliss in living over the past. Trust me, my dear Mr. Whitechoker, to look after him. He and my mother and my life are all I have."

The Idiot left the room, and Mr. Pedagog put in a greater part of the next half-hour in making personal statements to the remaining boarders to the effect that the word he used was eschewed, and not the one attributed to him by the Idiot.

Strange to say, most of them were already aware of that fact.

X

"THE progress of invention in this country has been very remarkable," said Mr. Pedagog, as he turned his attention from a scientific weekly he had been reading to a towering pile of buckwheat cakes that Mary had just brought in. "An Englishman has just discovered a means by which a ship in distress at sea can write for help on the clouds."

"Extraordinary!" said Mr. Whitechoker.

"It might be more so," observed the Idiot, coaxing the platterful of cakes out of the School-Master's reach by a dextrous movement of his hand. "And it will be more so some day. The time is coming when the moon itself will be used by some enterprising American to advertise his soap business. I haven't any doubt that the next fifty years will develop a stereopticon by means of which a picture of a certain brand of cigar may be projected through space until it seems to be held between the teeth of the man in the moon, with a printed legend below it stating that this is *Tooforfivers Best, Rolled from Hand-made Tobacco, Warranted not to Crock or Fade, and for sale by All Tobacconists at Eighteen for a Dime.*"

"You would call that an advance in invention, eh?" asked the School-Master.

"Why not?" queried the Idiot.

"Do you consider the invention which would enable man to debase nature to the level of an advertising medium an advance?"

"I should not consider the use of the moon for the dissemination of good news a debasement. If the cigars were good—and I have no doubt that some one will yet invent a cheap cigar that is good—it would benefit the human race to be acquainted with that fact. I think sometimes that the advertisements in the newspapers and the periodicals of the day are of more value to the public than the reading-matter, so-called, that stands next to them. I don't see why you should sneer at advertising. I should never have known you, for instance, Mr. Pedagog, had it not been for Mrs. Pedagog's advertisement offering board and lodging to single gentlemen for a consideration. Nor would you have met Mrs. Smithers, now your estimable wife, yourself, had it not been for that advertisement. Why, then, do you sneer at the ladder upon which you have in a sense climbed to your present happiness? You are ungrateful."

"How you do ramify!" said Mr. Pedagog. "I believe there is no subject in the world which you cannot connect in some way or another with every other subject in the world. A discussion of the merits of Shakespeare's sonnets could be turned by your dextrous tongue in five minutes into a quarrel over the comparative merits of cider and cod-liver oil as beverages, with you, the chances are, the advocate of cod-liver oil as a steady drink."

"Well, I must say," said the Idiot, with a smile, "it has been my experience that cod-liver oil is steadier than cider. The cod-liver oils I have had the pleasure of absorbing have been evenly vile, while the ciders that I have drank have been of a variety of goodness, badness, and indifferentness which has brought me to the point where I never touch it. But to return to inventions, since you desire to limit our discussion to a single subject, I think it is about the most interesting field of speculation imaginable."

"There you are right," said Mr. Pedagog, approvingly. "There is absolutely no limit to the possibilities involved. It is almost within the range of possibilities that some man may yet invent a buckwheat cake that will satisfy your abnormal craving for that delicacy, which the present total output of this table seems unable to do."

Here Mr. Pedagog turned to his wife, and added: "My dear, will you request the cook hereafter to prepare individual cakes for us? The Idiot has so far monopolized all that have as yet appeared."

"It appears to me," said the Idiot at this point, "that *you* are the ramifier, Mr. Pedagog. Nevertheless, ramify as much as you please. I can follow you—at a safe distance, of course—in the discussion of anything, from Edison to flapjacks. I think your suggestion regarding individual cakes is a good one. We might all have separate griddles, upon which Gladys, the cook, can prepare them, and on these griddles might be cast in bold relief the crest of each member of this household, so that every man's cake should, by an easy process in the making, come off the fire indelibly engraved with the evidence of its destiny. Mr. Pedagog's iron, for instance, might have upon it a school-book rampant, or a large head in the same condition. Mr. Whitechoker's cake-mark might be a pulpit rampant, based upon a vestryman dormant. The Doctor might have a lozengy shield with a suitable tincture, while my genial friend who occasionally imbibes could have a barry shield surmounted by a small effigy of Gambrinus."

"You appear to know something of heraldry," said the poet, with a look of surprise.

"I know something of everything," said the Idiot, complacently.

"It's a pity you don't know everything about something," sneered the Doctor.

"I would suggest," said the School-Master, dryly, "that a little rampant jackass would make a good crest for your cakes."

"That's a very good idea," said the Idiot. "I do not know but that a jackass rampant would be about as comprehensive of my virtues as anything I might select. The jackass is a combination of all the best qualities. He is determined. He minds his own business. He doesn't indulge in flippant conversation. He is useful. Has no vices, never pretends to be anything but a jackass, and most respectfully declines to be ridden by Tom, Dick, and Harry. I accept the suggestion of Mr. Pedagog with thanks. But we are still ramifying. Let us get back to inventions. Now I fully believe that the time is coming when some inventive genius will devise a method whereby intellect can be given to those who haven't any. I believe that the time is coming when the secrets of the universe will be yielded up to man by nature."

"And then?" queried Mr. Brief.

"Then some man will try to improve on the secrets of the universe. He will try to invent an apparatus by means of which the rotation of the world may be made faster or slower, according to his will. If he has but one day, for instance, in which to do a stated piece of work, and he needs two, he will put on some patent brake and slow the world up until the distance travelled in one hour shall be reduced one-half, so that one hour under the old system will be equivalent to two; or if he is anticipating some joy, some diversion in the future, the same smart person will find a way to increase the speed of the earth so that the hours will be like minutes. Then he'll begin fooling with gravitation, and he will discover a new-fashioned lodestone, which can be carried in one's hat to counteract the influence of the centre of gravity when one falls out of a window or off a precipice, the result of which will be that the person who falls off one of these high places will drop down slowly, and not with the rapidity which at the present day is responsible for the dreadful outcome of accidents of that sort. Then, finally—"

"You pretend to be able to penetrate to the finality, do you?" asked the Clergyman.

"Why not? It is as easy to imagine the finality as it is to go half-way there," returned the Idiot. "Finally he will tackle some elementary principle of nature, and he'll blow the world to smithereens."

There was silence at the table. This at least seemed to be a tenable theory. That man should have the temerity to take liberties with elementary principles was quite within reason, man being an animal of rare conceit, and that the result would bring about destruction was not at all at variance with probability.

"I believe it's happened once or twice already," said the Idiot.

"Do you really?" asked Mr. Pedagog, with a show of interest. "Upon what do you base this belief?"

"Well, take Africa," said the Idiot. "Take North America. What do we find? We find in the sands of the Sahara a great statue, which we call the Sphinx, and about which we know nothing, except that it is there and that it keeps its mouth shut. We find marvellous creations in engineering that to-day surpass anything that we can do. The Sphinx, when discovered, was covered by sand. Now I believe that at one time there were people much further advanced in science than ourselves, who made these wonderful things, who knew how to do things that we don't even dream of doing, and I believe that they, like this creature I have predicted, got fooling with the centre of gravity, and that the world slipped its moorings for a period of time, during which time it tumbled topsy-turvey into space, and that banks and banks of sand and water and ice thrown out of position simply swept on and over the whole surface of the globe continuously until the earth got into the grip of the rest of the universe once more and started along in a new orbit. We know that where we are high and dry to-day the ocean must once have rolled. We know that where the world is now all sunshine and flowers great glaciers stood. What caused all this change? Nothing else, in my judgment, than the monkeying of man with the forces of nature. The poles changed, and it wouldn't surprise me a bit that, if the north pole were ever found and could be thawed out, we should find embedded in that great sea of ice evidences of a former civilization, just as in the Saharan waste evidences of the same thing have been found. I know of a place out West that is literally strewn with oyster-shells, and yet no man living has the slightest idea how they came there. It may have been the Massachusetts Bay of a prehistoric time, for all we know. It may have been an antediluvian Coney Island, for all the world knows. Who shall say that this little upset of mine found here an oyster-bed, shook all the oysters out of their bed into space, and left their clothes high and dry in a locality which, but for those garments, would seem never to have known the oyster in his prime? Off in Westchester County, on the top of a high hill, lies a rock, and in the uppermost portion of that rock is a so-called pot-hole, made by nothing else than the drop-

ping of water of a brook and the swirling of
pebbles therein. It is now beyond the reach
of anything in the shape of water save that
which falls from the heavens. It is certain
that this pot-hole was never made by a boy
with a watering-pot, by a hired man with a
hose, by a workman with a drill, or by any
rain-storm that ever fell in Westchester County. There must at some time or another have
been a stream there; and as streams do not
flow uphill and bore pot-holes on mountaintops, there must have been a valley there.
Some great cataclysm took place. For that
cataclysm nature must be held responsible
mainly. But what prompted nature to raise
hob with Westchester County millions of
years ago, and to let it sleep like Rip Van
Winkle ever since? Nature isn't a freak.
She is depicted as a woman, but in spite of
that she is not whimsical. She does not act
upon impulses. There must have been some
cause for her behavior in turning valleys into
hills, in transforming huge cities into wastes
of sand, and oyster-beds into shell quarries;
and it is my belief that man was the contributing cause. He tapped the earth for natural
gas; he bored in and he bored out, and he
bored nature to death, and then nature rose

up and smote him and his cities and his oyster-beds, and she'll do it again unless we go slow."

"There is a great deal in what you say," said Mr. Whitechoker.

"Very true," said Mrs. Pedagog. "But I wish he'd stop saying it. The last three dozen cakes have got cold as ice while he was talking, and I can't afford such reckless waste."

"Nor we, Mrs. Pedagog," said the Idiot, with a pleasant smile; "for, as I was saying to the Bibliomaniac this morning, your buckwheat cakes are, to my mind, the very highest development of our modern civilization, and to have even one of them wasted seems to me to be a crime against Nature herself, for which a second, third, or fourth shaking up of this earth would be an inadequate punishment."

This remark so pleased Mrs. Pedagog that she ordered the cook to send up a fresh lot of cakes; and the guests, after eating them, adjourned to their various duties with light hearts, and digestions occupied with work of great importance.

XI

"I WONDER what would have happened if Columbus had not discovered America?" said the Bibliomaniac, as the company prepared to partake of the morning meal.

"He would have gone home disappointed," said the Idiot, with a look of surprise on his face, which seemed to indicate that in his opinion the Bibliomaniac was very dull-witted not to have solved the problem for himself. "He would have gone home disappointed, and we would now be foreigners, like most other Americans. Mr. Pedagog would doubtless be instructing the young scions of the aristocracy of Tipperary, Mr. Whitechoker would be Archbishop of Canterbury, the Bibliomaniac would be raising bulbs in Holland, and—"

"And you would be wandering about with the other wild men of Borneo at the present time," put in the School-Master.

"No," said the Idiot. "Not quite. I should be dividing my time up between Holland, France, Switzerland, and Spain."

"You are an international sort of Idiot, eh?" queried the Lawyer, with a chuckle at his own wit.

"Say rather a cosmopolitan Idiot," said the Idiot. "Among my ancestors I number individuals of various nations, though I suppose that if we go back far enough we were all in the same boat as far as that is concerned. One of my great-great-grandfathers was a Scotchman, one of them was a Dutchman, another was a Spaniard, a fourth was a Frenchman. What the others were I don't know. It's a nuisance looking up one's ancestors, I think. They increase so as you go back into the past. Every man has had two grandfathers, four great-grandfathers, eight great-great-grandfathers, sixteen great-great-great-grandfathers, thirty-two fathers raised to the fourth power of great-grandness, and so on, increasing in number as you go further back, until it is hardly possible for any one to throw a brick into the pages of history without hitting somebody who is more or less responsible for his existence. I dare say there is a streak of Julius Cæsar in me, and I haven't a doubt that if our friend Mr. Pedagog here were to take the trouble to investigate, he would find that Cæsar and Cassius and Brutus could be numbered among his early progenitors—and now that I think of it, I must say that in my estimation he is an unusually amiable man, considering how diverse the nature of these men were. Think of it for a minute. Here a man unites in himself Cæsar and Cassius and Brutus, two of whom killed the third, and then, having quarrelled together, went out upon a battle-field and slaughtered themselves, after making extemporaneous remarks, for which this miserable world gives Shakespeare all the credit. It's worse than the case of a friend of mine, one of whose grandfathers was French and the other German."

"How did it affect him?" asked Mr. Whitechoker.

"It made him distrust himself," said the Idiot, with a smile, "and for that reason he never could get on in the world. When his Teutonic nature suggested that he do something, his Gallic blood would rise up and spoil everything, and *vice versa*. He was eternally quarrelling with himself. He was a victim to internal disorder of the worst sort."

"And what, pray, finally became of him?" asked the Clergyman.

"He shot himself in a duel," returned the Idiot, with a wink at the genial old gentleman who occasionally imbibed. "It was very sad."

"I've known sadder things," said Mr. Pedagog, wearily. "Your elaborate jokes, for instance. They are enough to make strong men weep."

"You flatter me, Mr. Pedagog," said the Idiot. "I have never in all my experience as a cracker of jests made a man laugh until he cried, but I hope to some day. But, really, do you know I think Columbus is an immensely overrated man. If you come down to it, what did he do? He went out to sea in a ship and sailed for three months, and when he least expected it ran slam-bang up against the Western Hemisphere. It was like shooting at a barn door with a Gatling gun. He was bound to hit it sooner or later."

"You don't give him any credit for tenacity of purpose or good judgment, then?" asked Mr. Brief.

"Of course I do. Plenty of it. He stuck to his ship like a hero who didn't know how to swim. His judgment was great. He had too much sense to go back to Spain without any news of something, because he fully understood that unless he had something to show for the trip, there would have been a great laugh on Queen Isabella for selling her jewels to provide for a ninety-day yacht cruise for him and a lot of common sailors, which would never have done. So he kept on and on, and finally some unknown lookout up in the bow discovered America. Then Columbus went home and told everybody that if it hadn't been for his own eagle eye emigration wouldn't have been invented, and world's fairs would have been local institutions. Then they got up a parade in which the King and Queen graciously took part, and Columbus became a great man. Meanwhile the unknown lookout who did discover the land was knocking about the town and thinking he was a very lucky fellow to get an extra glass of grog. It wasn't anything more than the absolute justice of fate that caused the new land to be named America and not Columbia. It really ought to have been named after that fellow up in the bow."

"But, my dear Idiot," put in the Bibliomaniac, "the scheme itself was Columbus's own. He evolved the theory that the earth is round like a ball."

"To quote Mr. Pedagog—" began the Idiot.

"You can't quote me in your own favor," snapped the School-Master.

"Wait until I have finished," said the Idiot. "I was only going to quote you by saying 'Tutt!' that's all; and so I repeat, in the words of Mr. Pedagog, tutt, tutt! Evolved the theory? Why, man, how could he help evolving the theory? There was the sun rising in the east every morning and setting in the west every night. What else was there to believe? That somebody put the sun out every night, and sneaked back east with it under cover of darkness?"

"But you forget that the wise men of the day laughed at his idea," said Mr. Pedagog, surveying the Idiot after the fashion of a man who has dealt an adversary a stinging blow.

"That only proves what I have always said," replied the Idiot. "Wise men can't find fun in anything but stern facts. Wise men always do laugh at truth. Whenever I advance some new proposition, you sit up there next to Mrs. Pedagog and indulge in tutt-tutterances of the most intolerant sort. If you had been one of the wise men of Columbus's time there isn't any doubt in my mind that when Columbus said the earth was round, you'd have remarked tutt, tutt, in Spanish." There was silence for a minute, and then the Idiot began again. "There's another point about this whole business that makes me tired," he said. "It only goes to prove the conceit of these Europeans. Here was a great continent inhabited by countless people. A European comes over here and is said to be the discoverer of America and is glorified. Statues of him are scattered broadcast all over the world. Pictures of him are printed in the newspapers and magazines. A dozen different varieties of portraits of him are printed on postage-stamps as big as circus posters—and all for what? Because he discovered a land that millions of Indians had known about for centuries. On the other hand, when Columbus goes back to Spain several of the native Americans trust their precious lives to his old tubs. One of these savages must have been the first American to discover Europe. Where are the statues of the Indian who discovered Europe? Where are the postage-stamps showing how he looked on the day when Europe first struck his vision? Where is anybody spending a billion of dollars getting up a world's fair in commemoration of Lo's discovery of Europe?"

"He didn't know it was Europe," said the Bibliomaniac.

"Columbus didn't know this was America," retorted the Idiot. "In fact, Columbus didn't know anything. He didn't know any better than to write a letter to Queen Isabella and mail it in a keg that never turned up. He didn't even know how to steer his old boat into a real solid continent, instead of getting ten days on the island. He was an awfully wise man. He saw an island swarming with Indians, and said, 'Why, this must be India!' And worst of all, if his pictures mean anything, he didn't even know enough to choose his face and stick to it. Don't talk Columbus to me unless you want to prove that luck is the greatest factor of success."

"Ill-luck is sometimes a factor of success," said Mr. Pedagog. "You are a success as an Idiot, which appears to me to be extremely unfortunate."

"I don't know about that," said the Idiot. "I adapt myself to my company, and of course—"

"Then you are a school-master among school-masters, a lawyer among lawyers, and so forth?" queried the Bibliomaniac.

"What are you when your company is made up of widely diverse characters?" asked Mr. Brief before the Idiot had a chance to reply to the Bibliomaniac's question.

"I try to be a widely diverse character myself."

"And, trying to sit on many stools, fall and become just an Idiot," said Mr. Pedagog.

"That's according to the way you look at it. I put my company to the test in the crucible of my mind. I analyze the characters of all about me, and whatever quality predominates in the precipitate, that I become. Thus in the presence of my employer and his office-boy I become a mixture of both—something of the employer, something of an office-boy. I run errands for my employer, and boss the office-boy. With you gentlemen I go through the same process. The Bibliomaniac, the School-Master, Mr. Brief, and the rest of you have been cast into the crucible, and I have tried to approximate the result."

"And are an Idiot," said the School-Master.

"It is your own name for me, gentlemen,"

returned the Idiot. "I presume you have recognized your composite self, and have chosen the title accordingly."

"You were a little hard on me this morning, weren't you?" asked the genial old gentleman who occasionally imbibed, that evening, when he and the Idiot were discussing the morning's chat. "I didn't like to say anything about it, but I don't think you ought to have thrown me into the crucible with the rest."

"I wish you had spoken," said the Idiot, warmly. "It would have given me a chance to say that the grain of sense that once or twice a year leavens the lump of my idiocy is directly due to the ingredient furnished by yourself. Here's to you, old man. If you and I lived alone together, what a wise man I should be!"

And then the genial old gentleman went to the cupboard and got out a bottle of port-wine that he had been preserving in cobwebs for ten years. This he opened, and as he did so he said, "I've been keeping this for years, my boy. It was dedicated in my youth to the thirst of the first man who truly appreciated me. Take it all."

"I'll divide with you," returned the Idiot, with a smile. "For really, old fellow, I think you—ah—I think you appreciate yourself as much as I do."

"JANITORS HAVE TO BE SEEN TO"

XII

"I WONDER what it costs to run a flat?" said the Idiot, stirring his coffee with the salt-spoon — a proceeding which seemed to indicate that he was thinking of something else.

"Don't you keep an expense account?" asked the Bibliomaniac, slyly.

"Hee-hee!" laughed Mrs. Pedagog.

"First-rate joke," said the Idiot, with a smile. "But really, now, I should like to know for how little an apartment could be run. I am interested."

Mrs. Pedagog stopped laughing at once. The Idiot's words were ominous. She did not always like his views, but she did like his money, and she was not at all anxious to lose him as a boarder.

"It's very expensive," she said, firmly. "I shouldn't ever advise any one to undertake living in a flat. Rents are high. Butcher bills are enormous, because the butchers have to pay commissions, not only to the cook, so that she'll use twice as much lard as she can, and give away three or four times as much to the poor as she ought, but janitors have to be seen to, and elevator-boys, and all that. Groceries come high for the same reason. Oh, no! Flat life isn't the life for anybody, I say. Give me a good, first-class boarding-house. Am I not right, John?"

"Yes, indeed," said Mr. Pedagog. "Every time. I lived in a flat once, and it was an awful nuisance. Above me lived a dancing-master who gave lessons at every hour of the day in the room directly over my study, so that I was always being disturbed at my work, while below me was a music-teacher who was practising all night, so that I could hardly sleep. Worst of all, on the same floor with me was a miserable person of convivial tendencies, who always mistook my door for his when he came home after midnight, and who gave some quite estimable people two floors below to believe that it was I, and not he, who sang comic songs between three and four o'clock in the morning. There has not been too much love lost between the Idiot and myself, but I cannot be so vindictive as to recommend him to live in a flat."

"I can bear testimony to the same effect," put in Mr. Brief, who was two weeks in arrears, and anxious to conciliate his landlady.

"Testimony to the effect that Mr. Pedagog sang comic songs in the early morning?" said the Idiot. "Nonsense! I don't believe it. I have lived in this house for two years with Mr. Pedagog, and I've never heard him raise his voice in song yet."

"I didn't mean anything of the sort," retorted Mr. Brief. "You know I didn't."

"Don't apologize to me," said the Idiot. "Apologize to Mr. Pedagog. He is the man you have wronged."

"What did he say?" put in Mr. Pedagog, with a stern look at Mr. Brief. "I didn't hear what he said."

"I didn't say anything," said the lawyer, "except that I could bear testimony to the effect that your experience with flat life was similar to mine. This young person, with his customary nerve, tries to make it appear that I said you sang comic songs in the early morning."

"I try to do nothing of the sort," said the Idiot. "I simply expressed my belief that in spite of what you said Mr. Pedagog was innocent, and I do so because my experience with him has taught me that he is not the kind of man who would do that sort of thing. He has neither time, voice, nor inclination. He has an ear—two of them, in fact—and an impressionable mind, but—"

"Oh, tutt!" interrupted the School-Master. "When I need a defender, you may spare yourself the trouble of flying to my rescue."

"I know I *may*," said the Idiot, "but with me it's a question of can and can't. I'm willing to attack you personally, but while I live no other shall do so. Wherefore I tell Mr. Brief plainly, and to his face, that if he says you ever sang a comic song he says what is not so. You might hum one, but sing it— never!"

"We were talking of flats, I believe," said Mr. Whitechoker.

"Yes," said the Idiot, "and these persons have changed it from flat talk to sharp talk."

"Well, anyhow," put in Mr. Brief, "I lived in a flat once, and it was anything but pleasant. I lost a case once for the simple and only reason that I lived in a flat. It was a case that required a great deal of strategy on my part, and I invited my client to my home to unfold my plan of action. I got interested in the scheme as I unfolded it, and spoke in my usual impassioned manner, as though addressing a jury, and, would you believe it, the opposing counsel happened to be visiting a friend on the next floor, and my eloquence floated up through the air-shaft, and gave our whole plan of action away. We were routed on the point we had supposed would pierce the enemy's armor and lay him at our feet, for the wholly simple reason that that abominable air-shaft had made my strategic move a matter of public knowledge."

"That's a good idea for a play," said the Idiot. "A roaring farce could be built up on that basis. Villain and accomplice on one floor, innocent victim on floor above. Plot floats up air-shaft. Innocent victim overhears; villain and accomplice say 'ha ha' for three acts and take a back seat in the fourth, with a grand transformation showing the conspirators in the county jail as a finale. Write it up with lots of live-stock wandering in and out, bring in janitors and elevator-boys and butchers, show up some of the humors of flat life, if there be any such, call it *A Hole in the Flat*, and put it on the stage.

Nine hundred nights is the very shortest run it could have, which at fifty dollars a night for the author is $45,000 in good hard dollars. Mr. Poet, the idea is yours for a fiver. Say the word."

"Thanks," said the Poet, with a smile; "I'm not a dramatist."

"Then I'll have to do it myself," said the Idiot. "And if I do, good-bye Shakespeare."

"That's so," said Mr. Pedagog. Nothing could more effectually ruin the dramatic art than to have you write a play. People, seeing your work, would say, here, this will never do. The stage must be discouraged at all costs. A hypocrite throws the ministry into disgrace, an ignoramus brings shame upon education, and an unpopular lawyer gives the bar a bad name. I think you are just the man to ruin Shakespeare."

"Then I'll give up my ambition to become a playwright and stick to idiocy," said the Idiot. "But to come back to flats. Your feeling in regard to them is entirely different from that of a friend of mine, who has lived in one for ten years. He thinks flat life is ideal. His children can't fall down-stairs, because there aren't any stairs to fall down. His roof never leaks, because he hasn't any roof to leak; and when he and his family want to go off anywhere, all he has to do is to lock his front door and go. Burglars never climb into his front window, because they are all eight flights up. Damp cellars don't trouble him, because they are too far down to do him any injury, even if they overflow. The cares of house-keeping are reduced to a minimum. His cook doesn't spend all her time in the front area flirting with the postman, because there isn't any front area to his flat; and in a social way his wife is most delightfully situated, because most of her friends live in the same building, and instead of having to hire a carriage to go calling in, all she has to do is to take the elevator and go from one floor to another. If he pines for a change of scene, he is high enough up in the air to get it by looking out of his windows, over the tops of other buildings, into the green fields to the north, or looking westward into the State of New Jersey. Instead of taking a drive through the Park, or a walk, all he and his wife need to do is to take a telescope and follow some little sylvan path with their eyes. Then, as for expense, he finds that he saves money by means of a co-operative scheme. For instance, if he wants shad for dinner, and he and his wife cannot eat a whole one, he goes shares on the shad and its cost with his neighbors above and below."

"Yes, and his neighbors above and below borrow tea and eggs and butter and ice and other things whenever they run short, so that in that way he loses all he saves," said Mr. Pedagog, resolved not to give in.

"He does if he isn't smart," said the Idiot. "I thought of that myself, and asked him about it, and he told me that he kept account of all that, and always made it a point after some neighbor had borrowed two pounds of butter from him to send in before the week was over and borrow three pounds of butter from the neighbor. So far his books show that he is sixteen pounds of butter, seven pounds of tea, one bottle of vanilla extract, and a ton of ice ahead of the whole house. He is six eggs and a box of matches behind in his egg and match account, but under the circumstances I think he can afford it."

"But," said Mrs. Pedagog, anxious to know the worst, "why—er—why are you so interested?"

"Well," said the Idiot, slowly, "I—er—I am contemplating a change, Mrs. Pedagog—

a change that would fill me—I say it sincerely, too—with regret if—" The Idiot paused a minute, and his eye swept fondly about the table. His voice was getting a little husky too, Mr. Whitechoker noticed. "It would fill me with regret, I say, if it were not that in taking up house-keeping I am — I am to have the assistance of a better-half."

"What?" cried the Bibliomaniac. "You? You are going to be—to be married?"

"Why not?" said the Idiot. "Imitation is the sincerest flattery. Mr. Pedagog marries, and I am going to flatter him as sincerely as I can by following in his footsteps."

"May I—may we ask to whom?" asked Mrs. Pedagog, softly.

"Certainly," said the Idiot. "To Mr. Barlow's daughter. Mr. Barlow is — or was— my employer."

"Was? Is he not now? Are you going out of business?" asked Mr. Pedagog.

"No; but, you see, when I went to see Mr. Barlow in the matter, he told me that he liked me very much, and he had no doubt I would make a good husband for his daughter, but, after all, he added that I was nothing but a confidential clerk on a small salary, and he thought his daughter could do better."

"She couldn't find a better fellow, Mr. Idiot," said Mrs. Pedagog, and Mr. Pedagog rose to the occasion by nodding his entire acquiescence in the statement.

"Thank you very much," said the Idiot." "That was precisely what I told Mr. Barlow, and I suggested a scheme to him by which his sole objection could be got around."

"You would start in business for yourself?" said Mr. Whitechoker.

"In a sense, yes," said the Idiot. "Only the way I put it was that a good confidential clerk would make a good partner for him, and he, after thinking it over, thought I was right."

"It certainly was a characteristically novel way out of the dilemma," said Mr. Brief, with a smile.

"I thought so myself, and so did he, so it was all arranged. On the 1st of next month I enter the firm, and on the 15th I am—ah— to be married."

The company warmly congratulated the Idiot upon his good-fortune, and he shortly left the room, more overcome by their felicitations than he had been by their arguments in the past.

The few days left passed quickly by, and

there came a breakfast at Mrs. Pedagog's house that was a mixture of joy and sadness—joy for his happiness, sadness that that table should know the Idiot no more.

Among the wedding-gifts was a handsomely bound series of volumes, including a cyclopædia, a dictionary, and a little tome of poems, the first output of the Poet. These came together, with a card inscribed, "From your Friends of the Breakfast Table," of whom the Idiot said, when Mrs. Idiot asked for information:

"They, my dear, next to yourself and my parents, are the dearest friends I ever had. We must have them up to breakfast some morning."

"Breakfast?" queried Mrs. Idiot.

"Yes, my dear," he replied, simply. "I should be afraid to meet them at any other meal. I am always at my best at breakfast, and they—well, they never are."

THE END

www.ingramcontent.com/pod-product-compliance
Lightning Source LLC
Chambersburg PA
CBHW032106090426
42743CB00007B/259